I0561839

What's Love Got To Do With It?
a city out of thin air

What's Love Got To Do With It?
a city out of thin air

Steven Schroeder

LITERARY PRESS
LAMAR UNIVERSITY

Copyright ©2016 by Steven Schroeder
All Rights Reserved

ISBN: 978-1-942956-22-8
Library of Congress Control Number: 2016935530

Book and Cover Design by Regina Schroeder
Cover Image: *Burn*, watercolor and oil on canvas, 24 x 36 [2014]
Font: OFL Sorts Mill Goudy

Manufactured in the United States

Lamar University Literary Press
Beaumont, Texas

Recent Nonfiction from Lamar University Literary Press

Jean Andrews, *High Tides, Low Tides*
Robert Murray Davis, *Levels of Incompetence: AnAcademic Life*
Ted L. Estess, *Fishing Spirit Lake*
Dominique Inge, *A Garden on the Brazos*
Jim McJunkin, *Deep Sleep*
Jeanetta Calhoun Mish, *Oklahomeland*
Jim Sanderson, *Sanderson's FictionWritingManual*

For information on these and other books go to
www.Lamar.edu/literarypress

CONTENTS

a city, by the sound of it
> to interpret language means to understand language;
> to interpret music means to make music
> —*Theodor Adorno*

1

music sounds
like language sounds
like sounds like time and time

again and time again
and time again

and what is said
again no

sign of a system
no system of signs

     a prayer
spoken again and again
and again and again with intention

broken

to understand is to mean

to make music

2

a matter of sound, a matter of sense, a word
we speak to be heard—to be
a city, by the sound of it

¶ This collection gathers eight lectures delivered over the last six years under the auspices of the Basic Program of Liberal Education for Adults at the University of Chicago's Graham School. Six were delivered as part of the First Friday Lecture Series at the Chicago Cultural Center, and two were delivered at Basic Program Spring retreats.

Although I didn't set out to write a *series* of lectures, it became clear to me as I spoke with students and colleagues after the most recent (and most autobiographical) that this is exactly what I had done. Beginning with the first lecture in 2009, all of these pieces dance around politics, place, poetry, and vision. While the most recent talk doesn't bring that dance to a close, it does serve as a perch from which to look back on the others and perhaps shed some light on concepts that are of continuing interest for those engaged in one way or another in poetry and politics (and that, I'm inclined to think, includes us all).

A lecture is a public reading, a chance to think out loud in a disciplined way with an audience that is actively and critically engaged. It is, by its very nature, an occasional piece—a scholarly work, but not simply an academic one in the usual sense. As a performance, it is a talk at the same time that it is a written work. With that in mind, I've kept revisions to a minimum and tried to preserve as much as I can of the aural dimension. Notes and references are arranged at the end and are not explicitly signaled in the text (unless the reference was noted as part of the text itself, as is sometimes the case in a lecture). I hope readers will feel free to read straight through or to move back and forth between notes and text (and/or within notes and text).

For me, this is a conversation with participants who are coming and going. Feel free to interrupt.

The book is bound (as books are), but I invite readers to open it in a variety of ways—and join me in the ongoing work of unbinding. Carry on.

Steven Schroeder
Chicago
7 March 2016

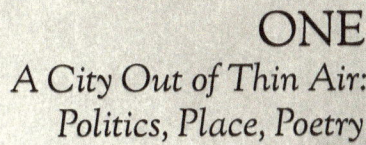

ONE
A City Out of Thin Air:
Politics, Place, Poetry

¶In preparation for this lecture, I went home to Texas to spend a week with my mother, who introduced me to poetry (and, though she probably wouldn't admit it, to politics) when I was quite young, via Emily Dickinson:

I'm nobody! Who are you?
Are you nobody, too?
Then there's a pair of us—don't tell!
They'd banish us, you know.

How dreary to be somebody!
How public, like a frog
To tell your name the livelong day
To an admiring bog!

—a poem that I would call quintessentially political.

Mom was then, and is now, convinced that a poem must rhyme. If it doesn't rhyme, it isn't a poem. And the rhyme she has in mind is end rhyme, rhyme time after time on the last word of one line or another. Despite her affection for Emily Dickinson's poetry, Mom is suspicious of slant rhyme: "rhyme" and "time" yes—but "line" breaks the pattern that breaks words to make lines at words that rhyme. She wouldn't buy "day" and the "dy" of "somebody" as end rhyme. In general (though she might balk at the comparison), Mom is more inclined to side with Malcolm X than with Emily Dickinson: *make it plain*, not *tell the truth but tell it slant*.

And, as my mother reminded me on this visit, anything having anything to do with politics makes her sick at her stomach (though she has told me she voted for Adlai Stevenson for president twice, and I suspect that she was one of the—I believe—six people in Oldham County, Texas, who voted for George McGovern in 1972). The perfect person with whom to discuss politics in some free variation on vers libre, don't you think?

To say that someone has gone to Texas (conventionally shortened to gtt) means they've suddenly disappeared without a trace—vanished into thin air. I mention this because when I'm gtt, more often than not, I'm reminding myself of the forces—social and natural—that first formed my eyes, that shaped my perception—meaning also the eyes I bring to poetry and politics.

I begin, then, gone to Texas, with politics and poetry.

II

¶ *Politics* is worn as thin by mindless repetition as by abstraction. We are awash in practices that go without saying, up to our ears in theories that do nothing but. When something goes without saying, it is safe to say it goes unchallenged. While it is safe to say it goes unchallenged, challenging it by saying may not be. To say it goes unchallenged is to theorize an other's practice—or one's own practice as the practice of an other—a practice itself, that places what an other does, puts an other in his or her place. To challenge, which takes place, one must take a stand. Both take place in *placing*.

[A reader of the previous paragraph will note (as I did reading it) that *politics* is italicized, a conventional means by which to emphasize a word. In hypertext markup language, for example, the tag , for emphasis, may signal that the text to follow is to be rendered in italics until turns emphasis off. But the tag may also be rendered by other visual signals and typographic conventions—an asterisk before and after, for example, which may mean no more to a reader than and . Rendering it in speech is another matter. There is, by the way, a separate tag specific to italics, but that is not my concern for now. And speaking it? I might raise the volume of my voice, I might pause for emphasis—or I might put quotes around it with my fingers.]

All designed to direct attention to the word, not the thing it names (in this case, an act—perhaps, in time, a practice).

It is the *word* that is worn thin by repetition—both the repetition of the word and the repetition of the practice (which is, by the way, a repetition of an act) it names. Repetition of the name of the repetition of the act wears the name, the practice, and the designated act repeated thin.

When someone says "that's just politics," it strikes me the same way as "he's only human." I think I understand the idioms, but I always want to say "if only she were *more* human, if only it were more *just*..."

In writing, I ended with an ellipsis. Did you hear it? And I might have chosen to stress *only*, or to stress *more* in both cases...

Ellipsis indicates something unsaid, something that will go without saying. Because it will go without saying, it will, in practice, mean saying nothing. And that, as John Cage reminded us, is poetry, if we say it now.

And therein lies a clue: here, the plot thickens.

When I say *politics* (both the word and the practice it designates) is worn thin, I mean that it too narrowly circumscribes both the semantic range of the word and the sphere of the action it designates.

Together, *if only he were more human, if only it were more just*, rivet our attention on the sphere of human justice—which we know from our reading of Greek literature as the *polis*. Our encounter with Greek thinking leads us to think this the place where humanity is possible. In this place, we may be human. In this place, humanity takes place. It is the place of which we speak when we say "political," and it is the place wherein we act when we do politics. This is properly circular: saying is a kind of doing, and doing is a kind of saying.

If Plato's Socrates is correct, we must ask whether and when this saying and doing is *just* politics. When we draw the circle too close, we wear politics thin. Poetry, on edge, is in the right place to thicken it.

I say "on edge" with bell hooks' account of the margin as a place of radical openness in mind, but also with an eye on *choosing*, which is almost always associated with freedom. To choose the margin, hooks says, is radically different from being marginalized.

Yes and no.

Thinking both vis-à-vis the margin is critical to thinking through poetry's place without simply placing poetry or putting poets in their place, as Plato is often accused of doing. But it is also critical to a politics of poetry that does not reduce poetry to a political tool (a variation on the theme of putting poets in their place).

III

¶I've already cited one poem as quintessentially political. Here's another, "Politics," by Miller Williams:

Mowing the lawn, having done with a tangle
of briar, with hornets buzzing in the eaves,
he is imposing order, but he leaves
some ragged grass where fences make an angle,
trapping a small shadow most of the day.
There, in the swarming morning, circling twice,

his dog turns herself intently clockwise
then drops on the flattened grass. In this way
she reshapes the world to suit a hound.
A square yard of his yard he leaves to her
because he sees that both of them are bound
as Jesus, Jefferson, Caesar were
(as all people are, and some small friends)
to change a stubborn world to fit their ends.

I am always puzzled when poets and others who otherwise love poetry say "I don't like political poems." I am equally puzzled when activists criticize a poem or a poet for not being political enough, particularly when they evoke images of retreat to aesthetics. I suppose the two examples I've offered so far provide some insight into why I'm puzzled: my quintessentially political poems may not be universally acknowledged as political even when they invite that description (as Williams does) in their choice of title. Some readers are likely to see Williams's choice of title as a kind of joke (an assessment with which I'm inclined to agree) and then go on to say this poem is not so much a political poem as a dismissal of politics. But I think it is anything but a dismissal, and its tone is anything but dismissive. Jokes are often the bearers (or, perhaps more accurately, the provokers) of the most profound insights.

In this instance, I think Williams has hit upon a fundamental problem in our thinking about poetry and politics—one that may partly explain both Jean Paul Sartre's nausea and my mother's. It seems that we have a tendency to approach both politics and poetry as unnatural, as an imposition on the world rather than a participation in it—and therefore as sources of alienation. Miller's mower, one might think, is at war with the world (and this image of yard care as warfare is a theme of more than passing interest in my part of Texas, where water is not plentiful and lawns may be acts of defiance). But is he?

In what he does, he is imposing order; but also, in what he does, he is being human. Being what he is, he is what he does—in mowing, as in other activities. And in doing what he does, the poet is also being human, being what he is, being what he does. The mower's imposition of order, his being human, leaves space in which his hound can be a hound. Both "change a stubborn world to fit their ends," but they do it by circling until they can *sit* in it. And the mower is singled out for leaving the space while making his place where his hound can make a place for herself.

"Space," the phenomenologists tell us, "is transformed into place by dwelling."

The poet is circling, not sitting, and the circling, which invites us to circle as well, may turn us to "Jesus, Jefferson, Caesar." What sorts of places are their dwellings making?

Adrienne Rich has covered this territory in both her poetry and her prose. In "The hermit's scream," in *What is Found There*, she begins a meditation on a poem by Elizabeth Bishop with epigraphs from Wallace Stevens and Alice Walker. That beginning alone constitutes a conversation among five rather different poets (counting the reference in the title of the book), and it is a tribute to the subtle power of intertextuality in promoting or provoking the kind of turning Miller Williams seems to have in mind. The snippet of Alice Walker, taken from *Meridian*, is particularly relevant here: "I am a failure then, as the kind of revolutionary Anne-Marion and her acquaintances were. (Though in fact she had heard of nothing revolutionary this group had done, since she left them ten summers ago. Anne-Marion, she knew, had become a well-known poet whose poems were about her two children, and the quality of the light that fell across a lake she owned.)" At first

6

glance, this reads like a dismissal of the now famous poet's retreat from public into private life—and, more damningly, into the aesthetic.

What poems are about is an interesting problem in its own right. What the best of them are about is the being of what they are, poems. And that inextricably connects them with the being of the poet, who is a poet only in the making of poems. But even more interesting to me for the moment are the quality of light and the owning of a lake. In the seemingly offhanded reference of Walker's narrator to the "owning" of a lake, a crucial political question is posed (a question that, because of Henry David Thoreau's masterpiece, goes to the heart of American politics). What on earth does it mean to *own* a lake? In this case, at least, it means occupying the land the lake occupies—dwelling on the lake—in such a way as to make the light falling across it accessible to the poet. There are few things as critical as light to the work of the artist, and access to it has a profound impact on the place of the artist (both in general and in particular) in his or her society. If the poet's owning of this lake cuts others off from dwelling on it—or dwelling on the light that falls on it, then she has cut them off from a practice of art, and that is politically significant.

Rich asks what political *activism* is—not exactly the same question I have asked about politics, but close enough. It is, she writes, "something both prepared for and spontaneous—like making poetry." Yes, and like the flow of any artistic practice, a play of spontaneous creativity on a life of work: practice, practice, practice. And, at least potentially, a play that is a public thing (a *res publica*, the Latin title of Plato's collective dream of a just *polis*). She marks the difference between collective action and thousands of individuals taking risks in isolation, thinking of themselves as "individual rebels." But, she notes, "individual rebels can easily be shot down." (Think of the young man standing alone in front of a line of tanks in the famous photo from Tiananmen Square twenty years ago.) "The relationship among so many feelings remains unclear. But these thoughts and feelings, suppressed and stored-up and whispered, have an incendiary component. You cannot tell where or how they will connect, spreading underground from rootlet to rootlet till every grass blade is afire from every other. This is that 'spontaneity' which party 'leaders,' secret governments, and closed systems dread. Poetry, in its own way, is a carrier of the sparks, because it too comes out of silence, seeking connections with unseen others." To do that, it needs a silence to come out of—but it also needs the promise of a response when it calls. So it is as much about waiting and listening as about speaking, as much about silence as about sound, knowing when to stand back as well as when to stand up.

IV

¶People often ask me why I went to China, why I go to China, why I come to China—questions that are very much on my mind now, since I will be going again in just about forty-eight hours. In a pinch, when I suspect the questioner won't have the patience for an extended response, I resort to a phrase artists have often used to account for their wandering: *for the light.*

When I have a (more or less) captive audience, as I do today, I spin that out into a longer poem called "for the light" that is part of my own ongoing dance with place as it relates to poetry and politics.

1

I come to China to learn
to walk away. Gray
kitten on a branch beyond my reach
cries, and I cannot coax him down.
He knows there is nothing

I can do, so I walk on, and he falls
silent. I'd like to think he found
some comfort in my voice
responding to his cry,
but he is still

treed, and I have done nothing.
The world is no less dangerous
for my words. He will tell his story,
put his feet on the ground
when he sees the time is right.

2

I come to China for the light, gray
soft through everyday
fog. The fog of every war settles
on this coast—power
speed sound

cities grow thick
with it, slow
to the chill consistency
of honey, set.

Everything moves
at the sticky sweet speed
of deliberate light, still
time.

Some days sun
glows dull through clouds
waiting to rain gray light
that will fill low paths
looking for a way
to ocean they remember
where these roads are.

Some days it shatters
into ten thousand
red shards on subtle
mist, scatters
across a whole
sky yellow to red, settles
finally to earth as dust
some god might spit on
to make a new man
to be fruitful and multiply
bodies of gray light
on dry land he names
so the god will know
how to address them.

3

I come to China for silence in a wall
of sound. There is no
denying the fire in

Lhasa, no
words for it.

4

I come to China for the leaves, always
Autumn. Kowloon in March, water
mirrors gray sky. They drop
green yellow orange red white
as the water of the fountain
swaying with waves
passing, milling
where there are edges. A brown one
falls in the center, bobs, does not appear
to move. But it is clinging to the edge of a
crowd an hour later, earth tone patch of sienna.

In Shenzhen, they scatter across
every walk over paving stone drones,
ragas for all hours, with the birds
who will sing for concrete eaves
when the trees are gone.

5

I come to China for the children
who say *hello* because they
like the sweet taste of two els
when they roll them on their tongues.

They never answer my poor
ni hao ma? But I taste *hao*
sweet in their laughter.

6

I come to China for the tricycle flower garden
that pedals past on a claustrophobic boulevard in
Nanshan after a Sunday walk, palm tree almost tall
enough to shade the rider on the leading edge of a dozen
potted plants in red and white, fragrance of lilies snaking
between buses through the crowd waiting for a break in
traffic to slip through before the light turns.

7
A man writes in water
on the walkway that echoes
Nan Shan's silhouette
walking south to the harbor
on Nan Hai Da Dao.
I step lightly
between characters,
glad I looked down.

This text will not last,
but I don't want to be
the one who crushes it

walking on water
without a thought
before it rises
silent on morning
heat into air.

8
A woman in black
with long black hair
takes hours to water

every plant on
the square
by hand.

She knows them
by name, and they
bring her flowers.

9

No one goes anywhere for any reason

but for love, drawn
by circles of friends, driven
by circles broken.

There is no place
but this.

V

¶ To end a poem with place drawn by circles of friends not
for any reason but for love is to risk being accused of mere
sentimentality—though Plato established love as a matter for serious philosophical reflection in the *Symposium*;
Augustine (following Paul) and generations of Augustinians, including Martin Luther and Martin Luther King, Jr.,
placed it at the heart of ethics; and Che Guevara singled it
out as the only motivation for the true revolutionary. The
risk would be worth taking without them, of course; but it
is easier to take it in such good company.

It is the pervasiveness of love in assertions like Che's—
or Augustine's "love and do what you will" that makes
it most philosophically interesting. As embodied beings

whose being in the world demands that we cultivate what Miguel de Unamuno termed a "tragic sense of life," we are surprised by flashes of wholeness. But those flashes carry the incendiary promise of connection and transformation that Adrienne Rich locates in poetry and political activism. I am convinced that the incendiary promise of human action is precisely what saturates action with political possibility, the possibility of a city.

One of the most cogent discussions of that possibility is Virginia Woolf's *Three Guineas*, which insists (as King did later, for example, in "Beyond Vietnam") on the interconnectedness of struggles at home and struggles abroad. As a philosophical work, it synthesizes themes she developed throughout her fiction. As a work of fiction, it continues the process of developing those themes, proposing an alternative to the rule of the fathers that completes the argument of *A Room of One's Own*. There, Woolf pictured society as a factory that produces persons by putting them in their place and keeping them there, with Cambridge, Oxford, and the British Museum as departments. *The Years* extended this to include the family and the upper class social scene of parties as departments of the factory, mechanisms of socialization. The "rule" in *Three Guineas* is an alternative to the rule of the fathers that is also a monastic alternative to the mechanistic process it implies. The mechanistic alternative begins with human beings as raw material to be *processed* into patterns and places that maintain the mechanism and the relationships of power upon which it depends. The monastic alternative begins with human beings as participants in a process by which human selves and human communities are born and nurtured.

It's tempting for me to walk you through the argument of *Three Guineas*, but I'm going to resist—better that you read Woolf than that you hear my summary. What I want to highlight here, though, is Woolf's embrace of what she calls an "Outsider's Society" (an anticipation of Václav Havel's *parallel polis*) organized around four teachers of the daughters of educated men: *poverty, chastity, derision, and freedom from unreal loyalties.* These teachers are analogous to (and partly overlap with) the vows of the Benedictine Rule—poverty, chastity, and stability (sometimes replaced by *obedience*). "Broadly speaking, she writes, the main distinction between us who are outside society and you who are inside society must be that whereas you will make use of the means provided by your position—leagues, conferences, campaigns, great names, and all such public measures as your wealth and political influence place within your reach—we, remaining outside, will experiment not with public means in public but with private means in private." Woolf looks back to a primitive state of religion, which she identifies with the present state of the profession of literature: "the profession of religion seems to have been originally much what the profession of literature is now. It was originally open to anyone who had received the gift of prophecy. No training was needed; the professional requirements were simple in the extreme—a voice and a market-place, a pen and paper."

Woolf composed *Three Guineas* as a personal response to a series of mass fundraising letters, the kind that masquerade as personal notes. She concludes with a vision that I want to quote at length: "as this letter has gone on, adding fact to fact, another picture has imposed itself upon the foreground. It is the figure of a man; some say, others deny, that he is Man himself, the quintessence of virility, the perfect type of which all the others are imperfect adumbrations. He is a man certainly. His eyes are glazed; his eyes glare. His body, which is braced in an unnatural position, is tightly cased in a uniform. Upon the breast of that uniform are sewn several medals and other mystic symbols. His hand is upon a sword. He is called in German and Italian Führer or Duce; in our own language Tyrant or Dictator. And behind him lie ruined houses and dead bodies—men, women and children. But we have not laid that picture before you in order to excite once more the sterile emotion of hate. On the contrary it is in order to release other emotions such as the human figure, even thus crudely in a coloured photograph, arouses in us who are human beings. For it suggests a connection and for us a very important connection. It suggests that the public and the private worlds are inseparably connected; that the tyrannies and servilities of the one are the tyrannies and servilities of the other. But the human figure even in a photograph suggests other and more complex emotions. It suggests that we cannot dissociate ourselves from that figure but are ourselves that figure. It suggests that we are not passive spectators doomed to unresisting obedience but by our thoughts and actions can ourselves change that figure. A common interest unites us; it is one world, one life. How essential it is that we should realise that unity the dead bodies, the ruined houses prove. For such will be our ruin if you in the immensity of your public abstractions forget the private figure, or if we in the intensity of our private emotions forget the public world. Both houses will be ruined, the public and the private, the material and the spiritual, for they are inseparably connected. But with your letter before us we have reason to hope. For by asking our help you recognise that connection; and by reading your words we are reminded of other connections that lie far deeper than the facts on the surface. Even here, even now your letter tempts us to shut our ears to these little facts, these trivial details, to listen not to the bark of the guns and the bray of the gramophones but to the voices of the poets, answering each other, assuring us of a unity that rubs out divisions as if they were chalk marks only; to discuss with you the capacity of the human spirit to over-flow boundaries and make unity out of multiplicity. But that would be to dream—to dream the recurring dream that has haunted the human mind since the beginning of time; the dream of peace, the dream of freedom. But, with the sound of the guns in your ears you have not asked us to dream. You have not asked us what peace is; you have asked us how to prevent war. Let us then leave it to the po-ets to tell us what the dream is; and fix our eyes upon the photograph again: the fact... We can best help you prevent war not by repeating your words and following your meth-ods but by finding new words and creating new methods."

Throughout her work, Woolf identified and probed the problem posed by the difficulty of focusing on the present—as embodied in persons, in places, and in times. The force that she associated equally with war and with commerce at the end of *Jacob's Room* is largely an effect of the drive to be elsewhere, to be other, and (as her de-scriptions of conversion and proportion reveal) to control. This "unseizable force" is the force of occupation and of Empire; it *takes* place, and it puts others in their places. It is equally a colonial and a missionary impulse, most of-ten carried out for the good of those it seeks to colonize and convert. The alternative begins in the four teachers of the daughters of educated men: poverty, chastity, deri-sion, and freedom from unreal loyalties. The first three of these, imposed from outside, are instruments of oppres-sion, long employed against women and other colonized people. But as vows, these teachers become cultivators of non-attachment and integrity. Taken together, they may facilitate being present by cultivating detachment from social rewards that are also means of social control (other places and other times that are ends for which this place and time are only means). They may also facilitate being present by cultivating an integrity manifested both in the refusal to feign loyalty and in the insistence that the whole be present in every part even though every part is particular rather than universal. The Outsiders' Society is characterized by experiment with private means in private, but the experimentation blurs the boundary between private and public. The public is constituted in being *present*, an intensely private act.

Jacob's Room, Mrs. Dalloway, and *To the Lighthouse* picture persons as beehives—not a matter of each individual being analogous to a bee in a social hive, but of each individual being a hive or a swarm. Boundaries are fluid. They often overlap. They are constituted as the bees that make up persons range the wastes, drawn by sharpnesses and sweetnesses in the air, then haunt the hives that are persons—both themselves and others. Human beings, then, are radically social, social to the core. Society is not a collection of individuals so much as each individual is a collection of societies. The permeability and fluidity of boundaries problematizes them. *Orlando, A Room of One's Own,* and *The Waves* all address this problem by crossing boundaries (sex, sleep, death, bodies). They ask in one way or another how what cannot be denied is related to who *we* are (and *I* am). None of the boundaries (not even the ones that cannot be denied) are entirely impermeable. To cross them, one needs space and time, a room of one's own. (Oddly enough, that space and time may be constituted in the indifference of the world to artists like Keats and Flaubert. Where hostility replaces indifference, the space is diminished or disappears entirely as in Judith Shakespeare.) *Flush, The Years,* and *Three Guineas* move beyond private space and time to examine the economic (or aristocratic) distortion of persons and communities. Woolf expands her vision to suggest that one needs not only a room of one's own but also (to borrow the partly metaphorical, partly literal mantra of Radical Reconstruction in the United States) *forty acres and a mule*, a means of subsistence.

Human beings are social to the core; we need space and time in which to be present; and to be present we need space and time structured in such a way as to sustain our existence as our presence takes shape where we are, between the acts, here, now.

The boundary, Heidegger said, is the place at which we begin our presencing.

There is no place
but this.

VI

¶ I am almost out of time.

Those of you who know Henri Bergson (especially if you know him by way of Gilles Deleuze) know that this is the place where the risk of abstraction is greatest. So I conclude concretely by returning to rhyme and perception.

My mother's insistence that it isn't a poem if it doesn't rhyme contains an insight that is critical to the task of questioning the whole society. If, with Roman Jakobson, we understand rhyme as a species of repetition, we can put it to work as a pattern finding and pattern making device—along the lines of Miller Williams's circling hound, for whom changing the world to fit her end is not an abstract matter: her end is a given in the world, and circling makes a place in which to park it there. Settling is a material imposition of a pattern, even if the settling is no more than an old dog circling to sit.

But recall that I said earlier that the poet is circling, not sitting, and this can be an aid to vision.

It has been illustrated for me in the way the plains impact the forming of perception. Growing up on the plains, I was led to believe the city was somewhere else—and, by extension, that makes the city something else. This could partly explain the long history of the city as an enticing place that draws young people and others looking for possibilities. (As Wendell Berry says, speaking of rural America, we educate our children to leave.) It could also partly explain the identification of the city as a foreign place, a dangerous place, and the flight from the city that has had such an impact on the shape of the North American continent. The city is the place that draws those seeking opportunity and expels those seeking safety. And that could partly explain the spread of oddly fortified suburbs in the United States in the twentieth century.

But, as I mentioned at the beginning, that circumscribes the meaning of "city" in ways that separate it from the human experience of those of us who grew up in places like Oldham County, Texas. I have come to believe I was in the middle of the city when I was in that place, where the population density was (is) 1.5 people per square mile, as surely as I am in that place when I am in Guangdong, where the population density is 1,210 people per square mile.

You may think that's neither here nor there; but I see it as an intersection of poetry, politics, and place—the kind of intersection where folklore locates deals like the one Robert Johnson made (and that kind of deal is music to a poet's ear).

Which leads me, finally, to Harris Stone's *Dispersed*

City of the Plains. Stone speaks of basic images from the cultural landscape of the plains—a derelict windmill, a grain elevator, a barbed wire fence, an abandoned missile silo—each of which may be viewed "as a reaction to a problem, as an attempted solution." Built structures are responses to perceived problems—and that is as true of a poem as it is of a dugout on the plains or a skyscraper in Shenzhen. (And, here, a note to Plato is in order: expelling poets from the city is a bit like expelling architects, builders, and building materials. What happens next, as I suspect Plato, who knew that human being in the world is a problem, was aware, is likely to rhyme.) Stone notes that perceiving built structures as responses to problems raises a series of questions.

An endless series, perhaps. But, by way of illustration and provocation, I end with three.

The first begins with a map and continues through an encounter to the question: The oldest surviving Native American map of this continent, drawn by a captive called Miguel by his captors, includes a depiction of what is now known as the Texas Panhandle. It is the result of an interrogation. Miguel was carried to Mexico City as a witness in the inquiry into the failed Oñate expedition that continues to ripple through the region today. The map signifies the region by means of settlements and roads. People live in the middle of nowhere before the Spanish arrive, connected by well traveled roads: between them, they make a place that the Oñate expedition simply could not see. Miguel, like subsequent Native American mapmakers, used a scale determined by temporal experience rather than by an abstract system of spatial coordinates. The distance between two points is the time that it takes to get from one to the other; thus obstacles play a role in determining distance, and the distance between two points may change even if neither point moves. Miguel understood people getting in the way.

Edwin James, a medical doctor born in Vermont in 1796 who served as botanist, geologist, and surgeon on the 1819-1820 Stephen H. Long Expedition from Pittsburgh to the Rocky Mountains authorized by Secretary of War John C. Calhoun during the administration of President James Monroe, describes a meeting that occurred along the Canadian River in what is now northeastern Potter or southwestern Hutchinson County in the Texas Panhandle. A "large party of Indians approached in an irregular and interrupted line, which extended more than a mile, from the opposite bank. They had, as was evident, already discovered us, and their outriders were seen plunging into the river at various points, and several soon came up to shake hands with us. The foremost scarcely allowed themselves time to finish this hasty ceremony of salutation, when they rode to reconnoitre some points of bushes and patches of low grape vines on our left, manifestly to ascertain if the whole strength of our party was collected. The main body of the Indians crossed the river more slowly, and as we halted on an elevation near the point where they ascended the bank, the whole passed in review before us." James describes the whole party—composed mostly of women and children—as being on horseback. He writes that every woman in the group appeared to be responsible for the care of "a greater or less number of horses, which were driven before her, some dragging lodge-poles, some loaded with packs of meat, and some carrying children, too young to be able by their own strength to sit on a horse, lashed by their legs to the saddle, and riding on in entire unconcern." They stopped at the deepest part of the river to fill water vessels, which James describes as "of the most primitive kind, being formed almost without exception of the stomach or bladder of a bison or other animal." James consistently refers to the women as "squaws." The chief, he writes, "who was one of the last to cross the river, came up, and shaking us each by the hand, with some appearance of cordiality, invited us to accompany him a short distance on his route, to a place where his party would encamp for the remainder of the day and the ensuing night." James notes that communication was in Spanish, via an old man who accompanied the chief and served as interpreter. Through this interpreter, the chief informed them that "his band were a part of the tribe of Kaskaias or Bad-hearts, as they are called by the French, that they had been on an hunting excursion to the sources of the Rio Brassis and the Rio Colorado of Texas, and were now on their way to meet the Spanish traders, at a point near the sources of the river we were descending. They in their turn demanded who we were, whence and whither we were traveling, and were apparently satisfied with our answers, though as afterwards appeared, they did not entirely credit what we had told them of the purposes of our journey."

The members of the Long expedition were not at all certain where they were at this point. Their journey had been facilitated by a well-traveled road established by Indians who routinely crossed the territory between Santa Fe and what is now Oklahoma. They had jumped to the conclusion shortly after arriving at the river that it was the Red River "of Natchitiches," as James put it. When asked about the river, the Indians "answered without hesitation, that it was Red river; that at the distance of ten days traveling, in the manner of Indians with their lodges, (about one hundred miles) we should meet with the permanent village of the Pawnee Piquas; that a large band of Camancias were hunting on the river below, whom we should fall in with in two or three days. Having described to them the route we had pursued, and the great and frequented road on which we had traveled, they said that when we were at the point where that road first crosses the river, we were three days ride from Santa Fe, which was situated behind a low and distant range of hills, that we remembered to have seen from that place."

For James, this is an encounter in the middle of a desert on the banks of a river that is mostly dry and therefore unsuitable for navigation. Even as he speaks to some of the people who had helped lay out and maintain "the great and frequented road" on which he and his party had been traveling for several days, he fails to see them or the shape of their city in this "wilderness." While traveling on that road a few days earlier, he had written of constantly meeting with "the remains of Indian encampments; trees which had been felled with the tomahawk, and other evidences that the country had been recently occupied by savages," and he had surmised that the shortage and the elusiveness of game resulted from the frequency with which it was hunted.

The meaning of *civilization* and *wilderness* themselves are posed as questions by this encounter. Here we have a well-traveled road, a territory more or less continuously occupied, established trade and trading centers oriented by familiar maps on both ends, a commercial language shared by many people, and established protocol for encounter with strangers.

Why, precisely, is this not a city?

The second is wrapped in a piece of a poem, Robert Frost's "Mending Wall," an encounter between two neighbors mending a fence that takes off from the old expression "good fences make good neighbors":

Spring is the mischief in me, and I wonder
If I could put a notion in his head:
"Why do they make good neighbors? Isn't it
Where there are cows? But here there are no cows.
Before I built a wall I'd ask to know
What I was walling in or walling out,
And to whom I was like to give offence.
Something there is that doesn't love a wall,
That wants it down." I could say "Elves" to him,
But it's not elves exactly, and I'd rather
He said it for himself. I see him there
Bringing a stone grasped firmly by the top
In each hand, like an old-stone savage armed.
He moves in darkness as it seems to me,
Not of woods only and the shade of trees.
He will not go behind his father's saying,
And he likes having thought of it so well
He says again, "Good fences make good neighbors."

The third, with which I end, comes at the end of another poem, "breakfast, near north," found at another intersection:

Smooth jazz
red, white, and rose
California wine promises

under plexiglass
on every table
announce conversations

with a *maître fromager*
on retainer
for people who love cheese.

Three words drift over
from the next table over
and over again: *Jerry Lee*

Lewis. Somebody
sings *somebody*
loves me. Maybe

it's you. Somebody
on a cellphone
says *Stevie!* and I

almost turn. Now
the conversation is
something about

a popular place
for second homes.
From the kitchen,

a woman's voice: *Que?*

TWO
What's Love Got to Do With It?
An Ordinary Song in Ordinary Time

¶The short answer, as I think Tina Turner knows, is *every-thing*.

But short answers are not the stuff of lectures, which are almost always more concerned with long questions that lie behind them and long questions to which they almost always give rise if we are paying attention; so I direct your attention to the three operative terms of the subtitle: ordinary, song, and time—four if we bear in mind that the second *ordinary* is no more the same as the first than is the second step one takes into a flowing stream. The subtitle, in a rudimentary way, illustrates one of the best known conventions of Hebrew poetry, taken up again and again in the *Song of Songs*: parallelism. An ordinary song in ordinary time is not a repetition but an echo in which the spin the second phrase puts on the first makes a space through which to see more clearly.

I'll say it again: the second time turns the first to open our eyes.

This second hand emotion has much in common with theology, which, as Gustavo Gutierrez noted, is the *second* step. What we are about, the matter at hand, is a second step—in this case, a close reading of a song that has been called (by no less an authority than Rabbi Aqiba) the holy of holies—holy, I believe, because it is so absolutely immersed in time that it determines the shape of the ordinary around which the extraordinary orbits. The extraordinary is nothing more than the halo we see out of the corner of our eye when we look closely and directly at what is there right before our eyes—nothing that is not there, nothing that is. And in this case, nothing matters, as it always does.

Commentators in several traditions (most notably Judaism and Christianity, both of which have claimed the book as scripture) have maintained that *this* song is the greatest of songs in the same way that the holy of holies is the epitome of holiness. That is probably true, but it may not be as clear as the commentators hope. We fail to get the point if we say simply that the holy of holies is *really* holy, just as we fail to get the point if we say the *Song of Songs* is a hell of a song.

It is, but...

The holy of holies is the epitome of holiness in the sense that it is holiness enfolding holiness, holiness all the way down and all the way up—so pervasive that nothing is untouched by it. And this is the structure of *shir ha shirim* as well—a song enfolding songs, a song made of songs, a song of songs that makes a song of everything. The holy of holies takes place by making space whole. The song of songs keeps time by making it sing. I believe this is more or less what Rabbi Aqiba had in mind when he suggested that "had not the Torah been given, Canticles would have sufficed to guide the world."

I am reminded of the great preface, the *daxu*, of another song of songs, the *shijing*, the classical Chinese book of songs attributed to Confucius (as implausibly, by the way, as this song is attributed to Solomon, and for similar reasons)—which, translated with only slight liberties, says

if you cannot say, sigh
if you cannot sigh, sing
if you cannot sing, dance

It's about time that we dance, so please turn with me now to a close reading of this text and let's see what spirit moves there. Poem, the *daxu* says, is where mind *goes*—so we attend here, where this poem is, to mind going.

There is a long controversy concerning the place of this book in the canon of scripture (in both Judaism and Christianity), and that controversy has often turned on whether this is secular love poetry or an allegorical representation of the relationship between God and the people of God. As is so often the case with either/or questions, the best response to this is probably *yes*. Anyone who can read a poem like

your kisses—I am drunk with them,
with your loving finer than wine,
with the scent of your sweet name

—all the girls want you—

take my hand, let's go!
take me, love, take me
like a king, to your room,

where we will laugh and drink kiss after
kiss till we are drunk with our loving,
with our loving finer than wine

—every one of them wants you

...anyone who can read a poem like this one, with which the song of songs begins, and say it is not exploding with sexuality has a better imagination (or more effective mechanisms of repression) than I. But there is also no denying that the relationship between God and the people of God has long been figured as a relationship between lovers—in both Judaism and Christianity as well as in cultural and religious contexts within which both have been thoroughly immersed. Comparative studies with Arabic poetry and Tamil poetry are fascinating on both counts, and even a cursory reading of Sufi poetry (including Rumi and Hafiz) or the work of San Juan de la Cruz and Teresa of

Avila demonstrates the possibility of poetry fully present to both sides of the supposed dichotomy.

By saying *fully* present to both sides of the *supposed dichotomy*, I mean to reject the tendency to reduce the secularity and sexuality of the Song to a sort of code or vehicle to be abandoned once we arrive at what really matters. The power of *shir ha shirim* lies in its clear eyed recognition that we have arrived at what really matters in the singers of the song and the singing of it.

I am reminded of Virginia Woolf's lyrical declaration in *Moments of Being*:

> "From this I reach what I might call a philosophy; at any rate it is a constant idea of mine; that behind the cotton wool is hidden a pattern; that we—I mean all human beings—are connected with this; that the whole world is a work of art; that we are parts of the work of art. Hamlet or a Beethoven quartet is the truth about this vast mass that we call the world. But there is no Shakespeare, there is no Beethoven; certainly and emphatically there is no God; we are the words; we are the music; we are the thing itself."

That is a philosophical and theological point to which I will return in a moment, but, on the question of canonicity, I am reminded of a line I first heard attributed to Martin Luther in reference to "Ein feste Burg ist unser Gott": Why should the Devil get all the good tunes? (and of A. E. Stallings' take on it, "Triolet on a Line Apocryphally Attributed to Martin Luther"). *Shir ha shirim* is one of the good tunes, and its place in the canon is a refusal to cede them all to Satan.

That takes me back to the philosophical/theological point made by Woolf, a point that I think is critical to the

Song of Songs: we encounter the extraordinary not in suppression or transcendence of the ordinary but in the ordinary itself. When she says "certainly and emphatically there is no God," she could be responding to a point that has often been made by those who say scripture is no place for poetry like that of the *Song*, which makes no reference to God. "God" is not contained in it. Certainly and emphatically there is no God.

And that is interesting in terms of a sacramental understanding of the secular. It should come as no surprise that an aniconic tradition like Judaism (and its offspring, Christianity and Islam) would recognize *absence* as critical to encounter with God. The *Song*, secure in the canon of scripture, sings what Thomas Sheehan, reading Heidegger, called "the absolute absence of God," the disappearance of God into humankind.

Where else would the *Song* turn but to celebration of humanity at its most human, and where else would it find that but in love?

By turning to love, the *Song* turns to human relationship at its most fully human. Coupled with the absolute absence of God, that *places* us—perhaps the most significant act possible from the perspective of ethics. And I am convinced it does this in both its form and its content. The form, in fact, is most significant in that it turns to song to make time.

Recall that *ethos*, customarily translated as *character*, originally meant a dwelling place for animals—a haunt, a place to which animals (and that includes us) habitually return. In Aristotle's *Nicomachean Ethics*, *ethos* and *nomos* are the two poles between which *hexis* takes shape to form a stable core for responsible action. Rabbi Aqiba's assessment of the *Song* suggests that we could make our way in the world with *ethos* even where *nomos* is missing.

The Song takes up *ethos* as *haunt* and makes that the center around which *nomos* forms in the singing of it. Human relationship—the human relationship of love—lies at the center, and that (forgive the cliché) makes the world go round.

Although this has sometimes been the subject of controversy, it is now widely accepted among scholars that the *Song* is not a single poem but a collection of lyric poems. There is still considerable support for the idea that this is a drama—more specifically, a liturgical drama—and that it therefore includes distinct characters in a narrative framework. But even among those who support this reading, it is generally acknowledged that the elements of which the book is composed are lyric poems. There is no denying some dramatic interplay among distinct voices in the book, but it would be difficult to justify calling it a play or a liturgical drama in its present form. It more closely resembles a collection of short lyric poems organized around a longer lyric that has a clearly narrative dimension.

Chana and Ariel Bloch follow this arrangement in their translation, as does Marcia Falk, though they diverge slightly in the way they divide the poems. I count 32, with the longest (and arguably most narrative) beginning at 5:2 and continuing to 6:3.

Let us turn to that poem for just a moment:

*I was asleep, but my heart woke
at the sound of my lover knocking*

*open up, my sister, my shepherdess,
my dove, my perfect one—
my hair is wet, soaked with dew*

but I have taken off my clothes
and washed my feet
must I get them dirty again?

my lover reached in for the latch
and my heart raced for him

I rose to open for my love
my hands perfumed,
their sweet scent on the latch

I opened for my love
but he had gone

my soul flew after his voice
I looked for him but did not find him
I called but he did not answer

the watchmen making their rounds found me
they beat me, bruised me, stripped me,
the watchmen making their rounds

swear to me, Jerusalem girls,
if you find my lover
tell him I am sick with love

how is your lover different
from any other lover
most beautiful of women?
what makes your lover worthy of our oath?

my lover is elegant and ruddy,
one in ten thousand

his head is pure gold
his thick hair raven black

his eyes like doves well set
on rivers of water washed in milk

his cheeks a treasure like a bed of spices
his lips anemones wet with sweet smelling myrrh

his hands are gold rings set with topaz
his belly is ivory studded with sapphires

his legs are marble columns
founded on glittering gold

he is like Lebanon
strong as cedar

his mouth is sweet—
all of him to be desired

this is my shepherd,
Jerusalem girls,
this is my love

where has your lover gone
most beautiful of women?

tell us where he has gone
and we will help you find him

my lover has gone down into his garden
to graze in beds of spices
to gather lilies

I turn to my lover and my lover turns to me,
grazing among the lilies

Clearly we've entered in the middle, with the "I" of the poem asleep. It is her *heart* that wakes at the sound of her lover knocking. We are justified in identifying the "I" as a woman by the lines spoken in another voice in the second stanza, beginning with: *open up, my sister, my shepherdess...* Here we have what clearly appears to be a dialogue between lovers. The speaker's heart wakes at the sound of her lover's knock in the middle of the night, and the lover calls for her to open, which she resists for a moment. Her lover reaches for the latch, and her heart races to him—again, heart first. The rest of her body follows, but not quickly enough. He is already gone.

Now it is her soul that flies after his voice, now silent. We hear her voice alone, reporting that she was beaten and stripped by the watchmen making their rounds—reporting, it seems, to the "Jerusalem girls," who function as a sort of chorus here. She asks them to swear if they find her lover to tell him she is sick with love—and that leads them to ask what makes him different, what makes him worthy of their oath, but also what makes him worth looking for.

The speaker responds with a traditional description of her lover's physical beauty in a mixture of natural and architectural metaphors. Duly impressed, the Jerusalem girls offer to help find him, but the speaker has already drifted off to her lover's garden, where they turn to one another, *grazing among the lilies.*

That interplay of intimate connection and violent separation—sudden, without a clear narrative development, permeates the collection—and it establishes the tone for human relationship as an interplay of intimacy and separation (or, in terms familiar from twentieth century psychological theory such as that of John Bowlby and Mary Ainsworth, attachment and loss). That intense blast of attachment and loss, with just enough narrative to drive the relationship through a rhythm in which attachment is followed by loss precipitated by violence only to return again, is, structurally, the center of the collection.

The first two poems, shorter and more intensely lyric, mirror this.

We've already looked at the first, in which the "I" of the poem speaks of drinking kiss after kiss with her lover until they are drunk—and in which a refrain that intimates the possibility of loss right in the middle of intense bodily attachment is repeated, with the slight variation that almost always marks parallelism in classical Hebrew poetry: *all the girls want you... every one of them wants you.* The body and physical desire are there right up front.

The second (1:5-6) intensifies the possibility of loss:

I am black, Jerusalem girls,
and I am beautiful—

dark as the dark tents of Kedar,
dark as the dark of Solomon's curtains

but do not see me as dark alone:
I have caught the eye of the sun

incensed, my mother's sons burned,
turned me out to tend their vines

but I did not tend my own,
I did not tend my very own.

What is perhaps most striking in this intensification of the possibility of loss is that it locates the beauty of the "I" of the poem in darkness that catches the eye of the sun. There is the violence that we saw at the center of the poem, and it is the violence of the brothers who, like the watchmen, are entrusted with the task of protecting the speaker—their little sister—but don't. And that leads to the powerful image at the end *but I did not tend my own, / I did not tend my very own.* We can anticipate here what comes at the end, in the penultimate poem, *my vineyard is mine.*

The last two poems (8:11-12 and 8:13-14) echo the first two, and this is indicative of the structure of the collection as a series of concentric circles around the image of attachment and loss in 5:2-6:3:

Solomon had a vineyard at Baalhamon
he gave the vineyard to watchmen
who brought in fruit worth a thousand pieces of silver

my vineyard is mine
keep your thousand, Solomon
give two hundred to the people who care for it

woman dwelling in the garden
companions listening for your voice
let me hear you

be like a gazelle, like a deer
in spice mountains

There is an intimation of a narrative in the forces that pull these lovers apart—and those forces, interestingly, do not come from outside the circle of their city. But it is the rhythm that carries the collection, and it circles around the woman dwelling in the garden.

That is an invitation to exegetical flights of fancy involving gardens in familiar myths of creation and fall—but it is also a lyric image of humanity exploding with the tension of desire.

As readers of the collection, we move from the first poem to the last across the concentric circles of the poems. It is our movement that imparts a sense of narrative to the collection—even if we end where we begin and begin again where we end. And that tells us something, I believe, about *tikkun olam*, mending the world.

After the first two poems, there is a series of short poems that take the form of dialogue (1:7-17). Where do you pasture, the "I" of the third poem asks, to which her lover responds by telling her to go where the sheep go and pasture where shepherds pitch their tents. He might as well have said "feed your life but don't get too attached to it."

This is followed by a series of lovely images anticipating the extended physical description in the central poem cited earlier:

I imagine you, my shepherdess,
as my mare among pharaoh's chariots

your beautiful cheeks framed in beaded braids
gold chains around your neck

we will make you rows of gold beads
with silver inlays

my king and I lie down
in the fragrance of my perfume

my lover is a sachet of myrrh
nestled between my breasts all night

a cluster of henna blossoms
from Ein Geddi oasis

...and then, again, rendering any attempt to reduce this collection simply to allegory, this exchange (1:15-17):

look at you, my beautiful shepherdess,
look at you—your lovely eyes are doves
look at you—my gentle, beautiful love

our bed is green,
our roof beams cedar,
and our rafters are fir

This is a celebration of a creation that is very good—but it is a celebration that is centered on *look at you, look at you, look at you*. Two lovers face to face are the center around which the world takes shape. Two lovers turning to embrace are the song that sings this whole song of songs into being, fully aware of the tension implied by the turning, in which turning toward always contains the possibility of turning away.

The tension of turning and turning, turning toward and turning away, is depicted most beautifully, I think, in the rhythm of natural and architectural images—including the one that leaps out of the thirtieth poem (8:8-10), just before the turn mentioned earlier in the penultimate poem, the declaration that *my vineyard is mine*. It recalls the failure of those charged with protecting the little sister of these poems in a quick exchange between the brothers and their sister:

we have a little sister
and she has no breasts
what shall we do for our sister
when the time comes for her to be spoken for?

if she were a wall, we would build a silver turret on her
if she were a door, we would bolt it with a cedar plank

I am a wall and my breasts are towers
but for my lover I am a city of peace

The poem begins with the brothers imagining what to do when their little sister matures and the time comes for her *to be spoken for.* These are the very brothers who, incensed with her, sent her out to mind their vines, causing her to neglect her own. Now they speak of her as though she is not there—*if she were a wall, we would... if she were a door, we would...* Her response, unsolicited, is startling in an ancient text: *I am... but for my lover I am...* This is a singularly powerful woman's voice coming from a woman who, by conventional standards, is not powerful. And, in a flash, it makes the assertion of who she is a political declaration: *for my lover I am a city of peace.*

The personal is political.

And the *Song* is a city. When we read this collection of poems, we walk from one gate to the other, straight across the concentric circles of song as though there were a linear narrative through them. That is a tribute to the anthologist, but it is also an artifact of who we are and how we think. (Not surprisingly, part of the history of interpretation of this book is an allegorical reading centered on the relationship between the active and the passive intellect.) Our thinking is narrative, but our insights, episodic, come in flashes. It is intriguing, I think, that this makes our consciousness more like an anthology (and I suspect more like an anthology of lyric poems) than a narrative. And, to the extent that we connect our consciousness with our politics (as we have been inclined to do in the west), it makes our cities more like conversations than fortresses or gated communities.

The little sister of these poems (who is often the "I" of the poem but may or may not be the author) offers interesting insight into the relationship between love and a city of peace (a relationship that was also of interest to Aristotle in his ethics, which, you will recall, was also a politics). Remembering earlier comments about the absolute absence of God, the disappearance of God into humankind, we approach this material mindful that the shape our humanity takes is most critical. Paradoxically, the absolute absence of God impels us to consider the kind of city in which God's presence can dwell.

So far, we have approached this city from opposite gates and taken a few steps in on each side. I propose now to circle back to the gate where we entered—with lovers drinking kiss after kiss until they are drunk with loving—and walk across the city to get a sense of how it is pieced together to make a city of peace.

From the starting point, we had walked through the first chapter, to that lovely image of a bed of green, beams of cedar, and rafters of fir. The images continue...

I am the rose of Sharon,
the lily of the valleys

as a lily among thistles
is my shepherdess among girls

as an apricot among wild trees

is my love among boys

I sit longing in his shade
and his fruit is sweet

...still in the form of a back and forth between two voices, still overwhelmingly pastoral. And then the chorus of Jerusalem girls is invoked, though they do not yet speak:

he brings me to the house of wine
his love like a banner over me

feed me raisin cakes!
scatter me among apricots!
I am sick with love

his left arm under my head
his right arm embracing me

swear to me, Jerusalem girls,
by the gazelles, by the deer in the fields

do not rouse us
until our love is satisfied

On the other side of this city, remember, these Jerusalem girls will demand to know what it is about the lover that merits their oath. But they appear at several moments along the way, like a link the anthologist has used to string these lyric jewels together. They are there again in the thirteenth poem, still silent, but the invocation of this eighth poem is repeated exactly. And the images between are full of action that moves us but doesn't move us from one place to another (2:8—3:5):

listen—the voice of my lover
leaping over mountains
doubling up over hills

my lover is like a gazelle
like a fawn behind our stone wall

peering in at the windows
showing himself through the lattice

my lover spoke and said

rise up my lovely shepherdess
and fly away with me

the long cold winter is done
the rain is over and gone

flowers blossom from fertile earth
and the voice of the turtledove
is heard in our land

fig trees burst with green figs
blossoming vines smell sweet

rise, my beautiful shepherdess, and fly

my dove concealed
in the crags of the cliff

let me see you
let me see all of you

let me hear you
let me hear your voice

your voice is beautiful
the sight of you is lovely

catch the foxes
catch the little foxes
that spoil the vineyards
that spoil our tender grapes

my lover turns to me and I turn to him,
to the one grazing among the lilies
until morning breezes rise
and shadows fly

turn around, my love
be like a gazelle, like a deer
in rugged mountains

in my bed at night,
I long for the one I love,
I search for him but do not find him

I rise and search the streets
and squares of the city for the one I love
I search for him but do not find him

the watchmen making their rounds find me
I ask "have you seen the one I love?"

soon after I leave them,
I find the one I love

I hold him and will not let him go
until I bring him to my mother's house,
into the room of the one who conceived me

swear to me, Jerusalem girls,
by the gazelles, by the deer in the fields

do not rouse us
until our love is satisfied

It is the turning and turning that drives the collection, the tension here between love and love satisfied—love satisfied, I think, being the city of peace (recall that Aristotle makes *philia* the glue that holds the human city together)...

The fourteenth poem (3:6-11) introduces martial imagery by way of a king's arrival for his wedding, accompanied by his well-armed entourage:

who is this rising like incense
from the wilderness,
rising perfumed
with all the spices
of a wandering merchant?

look! the entourage of Solomon
sixty of Israel's warriors surround him
each with a sword, each expert in war,
each with a sword on his thigh
ready for night's dangers

a litter made for Solomon of the cedars of Lebanon
columns made of silver, a chair made of gold
with a purple cushion, all made with love
by Jerusalem girls

come see, daughters of Zion,
come see king Solomon crowned
with the crown his mother gave him
on his marriage day, on this day of rejoicing

We return in the next poem (4:1-7) to a clearly lyric form,
back to the *look at you* of 1:15-17. Look at how this poem
evokes the beauty of the lover by drawing on the beauty of
the natural world, using a beauty familiar to the readers of
the poem (and hence place-specific imagery) to make the
singular beauty of the lover familiar.

look at you, my beautiful shepherdess,
look at you—your lovely eyes
are doves behind your veil

your hair like goats glistening
on Mount Gilead's slopes

teeth like white ewes coming up in twos
from washing in the stream, perfect twins

lips like double crimson threads,
and your voice is lovely

the delicate curve of your temple
behind your veil like a slice of pomegranate

your neck like a tower of David

hung with a thousand shields,
a thousand mighty warriors' shields

your breasts like twin fawns
grazing among the lilies
until morning breezes rise
and shadows fly

I will hurry to the mountain of myrrh
to the hill of frankincense

you are beautiful, my shepherdess,
all of you, no blemish anywhere

Place-specific imagery continues in 4:8-11—

come with me, my bride,
come with me from Lebanon
look down from the summit of Amana
down from the summit of Shenir and Hermon
from the lairs of lions, mountains where leopards prowl

you stir my heart my sister, my bride
you stir my heart with the glance of an eye
with one strand of your necklace

how beautiful your love is,
my sister, my bride—
sweeter than spice,
better than wine

your lips are honey,
milk and honey your tongue
your clothes carry the scent of Lebanon

At the same time it extols the beauty of the lover, the poem points to the beauty of her love, continuing the interplay of what is familiar to everyone and what is not. Love is available to all. And so the next poem (4:12-15) turns (as lyric poems do) to *this* love, which is

a garden enclosed, my sister, my bride
a hidden spring, a sealed fountain

your branches are an orchard of pomegranates
heavy with sweet fruit, henna blossoms,
the scent of lavender

musk root and saffron, sweet flag and cinnamon,
frankincense, myrrh, and all the best spices

a fountain of gardens,
a well of living water
streaming from Lebanon

This garden imagery continues in two short poems 4:16 and 5:1):

arise, north wind—come, south
blow breezes on my garden
let its aroma flow out

entice my lover into the garden
to savor its fine fruit

I come into my garden
my sister, my bride

I nip off my myrrh
with my aroma

I eat wild fruit
and honeycombs
drink my wine and milk

drink, friends, drink
until you are drunk with love

These brief lyrics lead to the central poem. The eight poems that follow, from 6:4—8:7, continue the place-specific natural imagery and bring us back to the image, already cited, of the city of peace in the thirtieth poem of the collection. At the end of the second poem in the sequence there is a sudden flight, the kind you might experience in a dream—from the familiar territory around Mt. Gilead to the chariots of Amminadid, where the "I" of the poems becomes the Shulamite dancing furiously. And the voice shifts with a question to that of the crowd of soldiers watching the dance, egging the dancer on:

you are beautiful my shepherdess, as Tirzah
beautiful as Jerusalem
daunting as the hosts of heaven

turn your eyes—they overpower me
your hair like goats glistening
on Mount Gilead's slopes

teeth like white ewes coming up in twos
from washing in the stream, perfect twins

the delicate curve of your temple
behind your veil like a slice of pomegranate

sixty the queens,
eighty the concubines,
countless the women

but my dove,
my perfect one,
her mother's only one,
light of her mother's eyes
daughters see her and call her happy,
queens and concubines praise her

who is that rising like dawn
beautiful as the morning
bright as the white hot sun
daunting as the hosts of heaven?

I went down into the walnut grove
to see the new growth along the river
to see if the vines had budded
and the pomegranates flowered

and before I knew it
my soul placed me
among chariots of Amminadib

turn, turn, Shulamite
turn so we can watch you

what do you see in the Shulamite

what do you see as she turns
between two armies?

how beautiful are your sandaled feet
o prince's daughter,
your elusive thighs
like the work of a fine craftsman
your navel like a curved goblet never lacking wine
your belly a mound of wheat in a field of lilies
your breasts like twin fawns
your neck a tower of ivory
your eyes pools in Heshbon by the gate of Bath-Rabbim
your nose the tower of Lebanon looking toward Damascus
your head like Mount Carmel
your hair like royal purple, a thicket that has entangled the king
you are beautiful, more delicious than all delights

Here (in the leap from 7:7 to 7:8), the collective voice of the soldiers watching the Shulamite dance becomes the singular voice of the lover describing his love—abandoning the martial imagery that would have him taking her the way an army takes a city for the slow (and thoroughly, intimately tactile) act of climbing a tree—not taking it, but placing himself in it.

you stand tall as a palm tree
your breasts like clusters of grapes

I said I will climb the palm tree
I will take hold of its thorny branches

your breasts like clusters of grapes
your scent like apricots
your mouth like fine wine

that goes down smooth sweet
whispering on sleeping lips

I turn to my lover,
his desire is for me

come, my love,
come into the fields
let us lie where the henna blossom

we shall go early to the vineyards
see if the vines are budding
see if the pomegranates have flowered

there I will give you my love

the air is filled with the sweet smell of mandrakes
and at our door every manner of new fruit
I have saved for you, my love

Near the end of this sequence (in 8:1-4), there is a poem
that turns again to the Jerusalem girls—but does it by way
of the wish of the "I" of the poems that the lover were her
brother—a wish that she notes would free her expressions
of affection by making their public display appropriate:

I wish you were my brother
who had nursed at my mother's breast

finding you in the street, I'd kiss you
and they would not despise me

I would bring you to my mother's house

and she would teach me

I would give you spiced wine to drink
my pomegranate wine

his left arm under my head
his right arm embracing me

swear to me, Jerusalem girls,
by the gazelles, by the deer in the fields

do not rouse us
until our love is satisfied

Near the end (8:5), the rising of "the little sister," the "I" of these poems, echoes the rising of Solomon *like incense / from the wilderness* in 3:6:

who is that rising from the wilderness
leaning on her lover's arm?

This couplet is followed by another short poem, a fragment, that puts the lovers together at the moment of birth, the one awakening the other, intensifying the turning and turning to make of this love a *res publica*—to make it the glue that binds the city, "the heart" in the words of another commentator whose theological insights are often overlooked, "of a heartless world."

there beneath the apricot tree I woke you
there your mother conceived you
there you were born

The martial imagery turns in 8:6-7 to the heart of the matter:

> set me as a seal upon your heart
> as a seal upon your arm
>
> love is strong as death
> jealousy as bitter as the grave
>
> even its embers are fire
> a fierce, holy fire
>
> no amount of water
> can quench love's fire
> streams cannot overwhelm her
>
> if a man tried to buy love
> with everything he owned,
> he would be utterly despised

The good news this song sings is that *love is strong as death, that for my lover I am a city of peace.* That song should suffice to guide us even where there is no law.

THREE
The Halo of a Veil of Tears: On Mysticism and Reason

¶Mysticism has often been equated with mystification and dismissed as irrational or anti-rational. But, following the lead of William James, Henri Bergson took it up as an object for serious scientific and philosophical study. Particularly in his treatment of mysticism as dynamic religion in the *Two Sources of Morality and Religion*, Bergson gestures toward mystical experience as a possible key to an understanding of human rationality that does not simply define it negatively as the opposite of emotion. In the practice of great mystics, Bergson sees a form of knowing that is more holistic than analytically circumscribed reason. This is rooted in his understanding of evolution as articulated in *Creative Evolution* and is particularly attentive to the relationship between instinct (most fully developed in the social insects) and intelligence (most fully developed in primates).

In the *Two Sources*, he expands this by suggesting that there is always a fringe of intelligence around instinct and a halo of intuition around intelligence. He connects mystical experience with intuition, which works as a force to drive intelligence in the process of knowing. Philosophically, he refers to this as "metamorphosis of dialectics into mysticism" in Greek thought, which he regards as incomplete. More complete would be an open-ended interplay of dialectics and mysticism which would take the form of a punctuated equilibrium—or, more properly, as Jean Piaget suggested, a dynamic equilibrium or *homeorhesis* punctuated by pauses rather than a final coming to rest (what James referred to as *perchings* in his discussion of the stream of consciousness).

Two comments by Bergson are of particular interest: first, that "complete mysticism is action" and, second, that "supreme good sense" is the mark of the great mystic. The emphasis on practicality is consistent with the epistemology and psychology of pragmatism. Connecting it with mystical experience points to a knowing that is not only practical but also whole, and that is promising. Bergson draws this into his discussion of "the mystic love of humanity," which, he says, "is not the extension of an instinct" and "does not originate in an idea. It is neither of the sense nor of the mind. It is of both, implicitly, and is effectively much more."

I find this consistent not only with pragmatism but also with Marx's description of the emancipation of human senses in his Paris manuscripts: "The eye has become a *human* eye, just as its *object* has become a social, *human* object—an object made by man for man. The *senses* have therefore become directly in their practice *theoreticians*. They relate themselves to the thing for the sake of the thing, but the thing itself is an *objective human* relation to itself and to man, and vice versa." When Bergson designates mysticism as dynamic religion, he points toward a religious function that is transformative rather than ameliorative—and, in his understanding, this is an intensely practical epistemological matter. Static religion is, as Marx lyrically described it, "the sigh of the oppressed creature, the heart of a heartless world, and the soul of soulless conditions. It is the *opium* of the people"—not a negative thing in a society marked by real suffering.

But *dynamic* religion is another matter, a call from within for "the abolition of religion as the *illusory* happiness of the people, a demand for their *real* happiness. To call on them to give up their illusions about their condition is to call on them to *give up a condition that requires illusions*. The criticism of religion is, therefore, *in embryo, the criticism of that vale of tears* of which religion is the *halo*."

It is, as is so often the case in description of mystical experience, a matter of seeing clearly.

¶In *The Varieties of Religious Experience*, William James notes four marks of mystical experience: it is ineffable, noetic, transitory, and passive. The first two suffice to distinguish an experience as mystical: mysticism is an experience of knowing that cannot be communicated. Because such experience comes and goes and does not last, James calls it transitory. But, transitory though it may be, it is utterly transformative. This one fleeting experience, undeniably particular, changes everything. Because it cannot be communicated, it must be *directly* experienced; and it must be experienced as *knowing*. Because it is fleeting, it is a flash of insight, a glimpse of a whole. That means it is not only beyond words but also beyond any one who experiences it. In failing, language points beyond both itself and its speaker; one may speak in terms of an *other* larger than oneself, wholly other. But in mysticism, one also speaks of union with that wholly other: in one moment, one *is* whole, and that changes *every* moment. What is a moment of mystical experience in ordinary language is, for the mystic, all there is; one moment of being all there is means nothing can be the same again.

In the light of Bergson's distinction between static and dynamic religion, it is less misleading to call the experience a *passion* than to call it *passive*. According to Bergson, what sets mysticism apart is its dynamic character; and this is consistent with accounts of mystical experience as transformative. When James calls the experience passive, he calls attention to its location beyond the will of the individual who experiences it. Mystical experience is ecstatic: the mystic, unable to contain herself or himself, senses himself or herself being carried beyond the ordinary by what she or he goes through in the ordinary. Something happens here now, but not because one wills it.

Bergson places religion as a social function in an evolutionary context. It is a matter of the evolution of intelligence, a social structure among other social structures that evolve in the same way biological structures evolve to facilitate being in the world. This is to say that structures, biological and social, are constructed across time within boundaries imposed by spatial and physical constraints which may themselves change from one particular place and time to another: all structures are particular, temporally and spatially bounded. Bergson sees evolution as an interplay of instinct (marked by necessity) and intelligence (marked by freedom) which divides into two main streams. In one stream, which culminates in eusocial insects (especially *hymenoptera*), instinct dominates. In the other, which culminates in primates, intelligence dominates. But instinct and intelligence are always present in both. Bergson speaks of a halo of intelligence around instinct in *hymenoptera* and a halo of instinct around intelligence in primates. Both eusocial insects and primates are makers of social structures that have a significant impact on their survival in the world. Bergson's focus on *hymenoptera* and humans is partly due to their spectacular success in supplementing social structures with material artifacts that have made survivors of them.

As Bergson understands it, *hymenoptera* survival has tended to focus on the group while human survival has tended to focus on the individual. This may be overplayed, but the point is to direct attention to the subordination of the individual in insect societies and the elevation of the individual in human societies. Interestingly enough,

Bergson believes that the elevation of the individual poses a particular threat to survival in humans while the subordination of the individual may also pose a particular threat to survival in eusocial insects. In broad terms, intelligence that too completely subordinates instinct leads to dissociation from the natural environment that is necessary for biological survival. All freedom no necessity means no body—which, in the end, leaves no place for mind. Instinct that too completely subordinates intelligence leads to dissociation from the creative activity that is necessary for adaptation. All necessity no freedom means no mind—which, in the end, leaves no one to make places and no one to take places that have been made.

For both Bergson and James, religion is a social phenomenon that is largely a matter of mind. But both point to perspectives in which mind itself is a constructed phenomenon that takes place beyond boundaries of individual organisms; and this is important both for understanding religion as a social phenomenon (in which individual behavior and experience are both essential) and for understanding mysticism as a variety of religious experience.

Marvin Minsky famously defined mind by saying that it is what brains *do*. While both Bergson and James would endorse the depiction of mind as both act and matter of fact (*pragma*), their analysis points to a more expansive definition. Bergson's *élan vital*, which has sometimes been misunderstood even by perceptive and receptive readers as vitalism teetering on the brink of teleology or aiding and abetting affirmations of faith in intelligent design, is one attempt at such a definition: mind matters because mind is what *bodies* do. Mind *is* where a body *lives*. And life is lived in bodies that are simultaneously individual and collective: every collective contains individuals, and every individual is a collection gathered into a system considered as a separate whole.

Religion is one place where mind matters, and Bergson draws a distinction between two ways—static and dynamic—in which it does so.

Ordinary religion is static, and it evolves as an adaptation to the detachment from craving for life that Bergson sees as characteristic of intelligence. This is not to say that intelligence is life denying, only that it is not entirely focused on survival. To the extent that it loses focus on survival, survival itself may be threatened. As Bergson understands it, this is related to the emergence of freedom out of necessity and is marked by a growing detachment from what is necessary in favor of what is arbitrary (that is, willed). That may be a partially positive development in terms of human consciousness, but it is problematic if it leads to neglect of what is necessary for biological survival. An organism that doesn't eat or reproduce, for example, doesn't survive. The evolutionary strand in which intelligence takes precedence over instinct depends on habit to ensure that necessities are attended to, and habit is institutionalized in social structures that extend biological bodies. We are, in short, embodied in our social structures, and, for better or for worse, we respond to social habits as necessary. Bergson hastens to point out that the necessity of habit is not identical to physical necessity: ignoring a social convention such as a speed limit would not have exactly the same effect as ignoring a physical necessity such as gravity. Step off a cliff, and you will fall. If the cliff is high enough, you will be injured or killed by the fall. Drive too fast, and you may or may not get a ticket. But social structures depend on individuals responding to conventions in habitual ways that treat them as though they were necessary. Static religion is one structure by which human societies have bound individuals to convention. It has functioned as a means by which to keep particular social bodies alive: it has preserved bodies politic by keeping other bodies in line.

This is where the description of religion Karl Marx articulated in his short (and doubly preliminary) critique of Hegel (an introduction to a contribution, he called it) enters. Part of the description, religion as "the opium of the people," is familiar; but the description within which that phrase is embedded is rarely cited. It is, to begin with, part of a criticism of Hegel, which, in Marx, means that it is a criticism of a particularly important variety of philosophical idealism. And it is a comment on "the criticism of religion," understood both as criticism with religion as its object and the criticism of society that religion, particularly in Germany, has undertaken historically. This should at least call to mind a Lutheran criticism (with roots that predate Luther) of religion that obscures what is essential by elevating what is not, a criticism at least partly motivated by the perception that one external ritual (the sale of indulgences) placed a particular burden on German peasants. Marx almost certainly had that criticism in mind when he wrote that "*Religious* suffering is, at one and the same time, the *expression* of real suffering and a *protest* against real suffering. Religion is the sigh of the oppressed creature, the heart of a heartless world, and the soul of soulless conditions. It is the *opium* of the people."

Keeping Bergson's argument in mind, the individual freedom associated with intelligence could lead victims of oppression in a heartless world to despair and leave it behind. A critical function of static religion is to keep such people bound to the world by mitigating the pain it involves and, in some cases, by tying their behavior in this world to a state that they believe will follow it. Marx recognizes that the provision of an opiate is a recognition of real pain, and it is entirely possible that the relief of real pain—even if it addresses only the symptom and not its cause—could play an important role in survival. But, by masking the pain, it could also divert attention from what matters. (This is Marx's gloss on Luther's thesis, responding to the sale of indulgences, that the call to repentance is a call to a life of repentance, not a release that can be packaged and purchased).

Marx's criticism of religion parallels his criticism of the State, and both parallel his criticism of philosophy. All three are intent on putting a particular social construction in perspective, enabling those within the structure to see through it rather than being contained by it. For Marx, religion, the State, and philosophy are not problems in themselves; but an inverted perspective on any of the three is. Philosophy upside down is idealism that results in mystification and utopianism. The State upside down is tyranny that results in alienation and oppression. Religion upside down is illusory happiness that diverts attention from the real possibility of happiness.

The problem posed by all three is that each shapes criticism in its own sphere. Because philosophy determines what passes as reason, criticism of the whole is irrational. Because the State determines what passes as legal, criticism of the whole is arrested. Because religion determines what passes as righteous, criticism of the whole is damned. More to the point, systemic criticism in all three spheres is liable to excommunication.

It has no place there.

III

¶ Despite the anti-idealist philosophical bent of pragmatism, Marxism, and Bergsonism, the revolutionary response to a structure upside down is a matter of mind. To turn it over is to make a place for radical criticism. Bergson's *intuition*, drawing on mystical experience that runs counter to the essential conservatism of static religion, suggests a place for critical practice.

As Gilles Deleuze notes, intuition is the method of Bergson's philosophy, as dialectic is the method of Hegel's. It bears comparison to the pragmatism of William James, particularly as it relates to *duration* and seeing whole. By focusing on *pragma*, James and his colleagues directed attention simultaneously to empirical fact and to action, both of which are included in the meaning of the Greek word. The fact or *thing* denoted by *pragma* is the completion of an act. It suggests the perspective of a whole that contains the action leading up to it.

But in the case of an action that is ongoing, the only completion is a moment rendered incomplete as the process continues. This is precisely the sense articulated by James in his discussion of the stream of consciousness in his *Principles of Psychology*. Wholes to which we have access are like momentary perchings in the flight of a bird, and this is reminiscent of the transitoriness of mysticism.

By associating intuition with duration, Bergson blazes a similar trail. Intuition marks the momentary apprehension of the whole process of an action; but, because the process continues, the apprehension is dynamic. Marx describes a similar process in his analyses of objectification and alienation. Looking back over a whole process of action as the construction of a moment may give one a clearer perspective looking forward: the senses become theoreticians in their practice, projecting a vision that is continuously modified.

In James's version (as in Marx's), knowing is a circular experimental process. Theory that emerges out of action on the world shapes action in the world which shapes theory again. Theory emerges where mind does, in the space between the actor and that on which she or he acts—which in this circular experimental process means not between an active subject and a passive object but between two agents acting.

Bergson's interest in mysticism derives at least in part from its pragmatic (as opposed to dogmatic) approach to the world. It is experimental religion, and the halo of intuition Bergson locates around intelligence means that the empirical quality of knowledge consists not in its fixity but in its active engagement. Complete mysticism, Bergson says, is *action*, and it is marked by "supreme good sense." An intuitive grasp of the world is not irrational or antirational. It is an actively cultivated ability to attend to the whole of the world in every part even as the whole evolves, and every part with it.

Bergson routinely points to the great Christian mystics as instances of complete mysticism. While this is partly indicative of an inadequate reading of non-Christian practices, it is also a useful starting point to the extent that it is predicated on an embrace of humanity in Christian mysticism rather than its renunciation, an embrace that is inextricably connected with the paradoxical wholeness Bergson's epistemology demands. This is critical to Bergson and consistent with Marx's critique, which maintains that "Religion is, indeed, the self-consciousness and self-esteem of man who has either not yet won through to himself, or has already lost himself again. But *man* is no abstract being squatting outside the world. Man is *the world of man*—state, society. This state and this society produce religion, which is an *inverted consciousness of the world*, because they are an *inverted world*. Religion is the general theory of this world, its encyclopaedic compendium, its logic in popular form, its spiritual *point d'honneur*, its enthusiasm, its moral sanction, its solemn complement, and its universal basis of consolation and justification. It is the *fantastic realization* of the human essence since the *human essence* has not acquired any true reality. The struggle against religion is, therefore, indirectly the struggle *against that world* whose spiritual aroma is religion." The struggle against religion, like the struggle against philosophy and against the State, is a struggle to see through them. In this struggle, Bergson maintains that the mystics are our best exemplars.

IV

¶The fourteenth century English mystic Julian of Norwich left two versions of a series of visions—*showings*, she called them—that she experienced when she was thirty years old. The first version, the shorter one, was written shortly after she experienced the showings in 1373. The second, and longer, version was written some twenty years later after a long period of prayer and reflection. The two versions are glimpses that provide an occasion for reflection on the development of vision (understood broadly as an epistemological term, a kind of knowing) in a mystic who saw her own experience both as a development toward wholeness shown to her and as a vision she was called to show others. Julian saw her experience as a complete embrace of humanity, including her own humanity and the humanity of God.

The visions occurred in 1373, when Julian was "thirty and a half" years old. Both the short and long versions begin by referring to all the showings collectively as one vision, suggesting Julian's concern to integrate the sixteen visions she describes into one experience. That experience began when Julian became critically ill at the age of thirty.

She describes the illness as going on for three days and three nights before, on the fourth night, she received the sacrament of extreme unction. That this sacrament was administered is an indication that Julian and those around her believed her death was imminent.

Julian sets her experience in context by telling us that she had prayed when she was young for this "bodily sickness" to strike her at the age of thirty. This was one of three *graces* she said she desired (the other two being recollection of Christ's Passion and *three wounds*), apparently because it would mean participation in all the rites of the Church and perhaps because of the unique perspective on life afforded by proximity to death. Julian's desire for three wounds was modeled after Saint Cecilia who, according to legend, died of three wounds in the neck from a sword. The desire to participate in all the rites of the Church and the desire for a perspective on life provided by death highlight the driving force in what we know of Julian: desire for union or completion—with the Church and with God. That she modeled her desire after the life of a saint is indicative of the extent to which Julian wove popular tradition together with her own life story, and it is illustrative of the effectiveness with which static religion—even in the life of a mystic—constructs artifices with which to bind lives together and to bind them into the world.

Julian's description of her near death experience is detached and clinical, probably reflecting her familiarity with standards applicable within the Church to determine whether a healing is miraculous. Concerned to establish the historicity of her account, she is careful to describe her illness as precisely as possible and to emphasize that those around her were convinced she would die. This description, juxtaposed with her sudden recovery, establishes the miraculous character of her healing.

Julian suffered on for two days and two nights. On the third night, she and all those around her were convinced that she would die. But she lasted until day, when she says her body was dead "from the middle downward." Those around her sent for a priest. He arrived with a crucifix and set it before her face:

"'Daughter, I have brought you the image of your saviour. Look at it and take comfort from it, in reverence of him who died for you and me.' It seemed to me that I was well as I was, for my eyes were set upwards toward heaven, where I trusted that I was going; but nevertheless I agreed to fix my eyes on the face of the crucifix if I could, so as to hold out longer until my end came, for it seemed to me that I could hold out longer with my eyes set in front of me rather than upwards. After this my sight began to fail, and it was all dark around me in the room, dark as night, except that there was ordinary light trained upon the image of the cross, I never knew how. Everything around the cross was ugly to me, as if it were occupied by a great crowd of devils.

After that I felt as if the upper part of my body were beginning to die. My hands fell down on either side, and I was so weak that my head lolled to one side. The greatest pain that I felt was my shortness of breath and the ebbing of my life. Then truly I believed that I was at the point of death. And suddenly, in that moment all my pain left me, and I was as sound, particularly in the upper part of my body, as ever I was before or have been since."

Julian's description of her dying and her miraculous recovery are important, but I quote this section at length to highlight her focus on the crucifix, which comes to symbolize the humanity of Christ. She later experiences the suggestion that she look up to heaven as a temptation. The humanity, she is convinced, is all she needs.

Julian's focus on the humanity of Christ is expanded in the long version where she insists that the whole Trinity resides in the humanity. Her emphasis on continual recollection becomes a *making present* in which the whole Godhead is experienced in her identification with the Passion of Christ: it is in her compassion that she experiences God's presence.

Julian's visions move from an intense focus on the humanity, particularly the Passion, of Jesus, through a vision of Heaven (then, in the long text, the Trinity) *in that* humanity and a confrontation with the seeming paradox posed by the existence of sin alongside God's identification with humankind (and the assurance that "all manner of things will be well"), to the assurance that God's meaning is love and that love envelops all.

She says she saw six things "in her understanding": (1) the tokens of the blessed Passion, (2) the virgin Mary, (3) the divinity, (4) everything he has made, (5) everything made and preserved through love, and (6) that "God is everything which is good, and the goodness which everything has is God." Julian indicates that she was given "space and time to contemplate" the vision: when the bodily vision ceased, the spiritual vision persisted. This corresponds to what we know of her life and her spirituality. We have no evidence of repeated mystical experiences of the type that occurred during this intense period of critical illness. But the visions persisted as a basis for years of reflection.

There is some evidence that Julian joined a religious order at a very young age (this would account for her impressive erudition evidenced by her mastery of rhetoric) and that she continued in this order until the long text was written, at which time she became an anchoress. This would provide a context for the reflection that led to the long text and for Julian's reputation as a spiritual director (evidenced by her encounter with Margery Kempe).

Julian's text is not written for contemplatives. She insists that everything she says about herself is meant to apply to all her fellow Christians: the vision is "common and general, just as we are all one." She describes the teaching as consisting of three parts: (1) bodily vision, (2) words formed in the understanding, and (3) spiritual vision. She implies that she can show the bodily vision in the words she speaks so that others can see the spiritual vision.

Julian wishes to see more. She is answered in her reason "that if God wished to show me more he would, but that I needed no light but him." She says that she saw God "in an instant of time" in her understanding. "I saw that he is present in all things... he does everything which is done... I was compelled to admit that everything which is done is well done, and I was certain that God does no sin. Therefore it seemed to me that sin is nothing..." She experienced a period of rapid alternation of joy and pain as a result of which she realized that neither the joy nor the pain is caused by sin. We earn neither, but both are from God's love.

Julian counsels against pursuing the pain that we experience as well as the joy. She feels the pain of Christ. She says there is no greater physical pain but that despair is greater, because it is a spiritual pain: "Those who loved him suffered pain for their love," she says, "and those who did not love him suffered pain because the comfort of all creation failed them." Julian sees her safety consisting in staying focused on the cross. She refuses to look away from it—even to look to heaven. The cross, she says, is her heaven. Julian says that love gave strength to Jesus's humanity "to suffer more than all men could... But the love which made him suffer all this surpasses all his pains as far as heaven is above earth. For his pains were a deed, performed once through the motion of love; but his love was without beginning and is and ever will be without any end." In the midst of her experience of Christ's pain, there is a sudden change to an appearance of joy: "And then cheerfully our Lord suggested to my mind: Where is there any instant of your pain or your grief?" Julian is lifted up to see three heavens, all "of the blessed humanity of Christ."

Troubled by the paradox of the existence of sin alongside the all-encompassing love of God, she is led to assert that "sin is necessary." But, she says, "I did not see sin, for I believe that it has no kind of substance, no share in being, nor can it be recognized except by the pains which it causes." She identifies "every kind of compassion which one has for one's fellow Christians in love as Christ in us." She is told that "Adam's sin was the greatest harm ever done or ever to be done until the end of the world." But God goes on to tell her that "since I have set right the greatest of harms, it is my will that you should know through this that I shall set right everything which is less." Julian says "when I first saw that God does everything which is done, I did not see sin, and then I saw that all is well. But when God did show me sin, it was then that he said: All will be well." Later she concludes that "no more than is his love for us withheld because of our sin does he want us to withhold our love for ourselves and our fellow Christians; we must hate sin utterly, and love souls endlessly as God loves them." Both sin and pain are nothing: "For all this life and all the longing we have here is only an instant of time, and when we are suddenly taken into bliss out of pain, it will be nothing." This realization and the vision of God's love inspire great confidence: "I am certain," she writes, "that if there had been no one but I to be saved, God would have done everything which he has done for me. And so ought every soul to think..."

Pass over suffering to know God.

Julian's experience follows the classical mystical pattern of purgation, illumination, union. She experiences the years of prayerful reflection between the vision and the writing of the long text as a progressive illumination, an illumination in which God's voice is heard apparently as much through her reading and study as through her more clearly mystical experience. The vision itself takes on a purgative quality as she experiences the pain of Christ's Passion and modifies her inclination to call on everyone to share in that pain.

The visions are (as Urban Holmes suggests) eucharistic in that they make God present in humankind. This is paralleled by an impetus toward union and wholeness captured most effectively, I think, in Chapter IV (the fifth chapter in the long text): "And in this he showed me something small, no bigger than a hazlenut, lying in the palm of my hand, and I perceived that it was as round as any ball. I looked at it and thought: What can this be? And I was given this general answer: It is everything which is made. I was amazed that it could last, for I thought that it was so little that it could suddenly fall into nothing. And I was answered in my understanding: It lasts and always will, because God loves it; and thus everything has being through the love of God."

Julian focuses on God's presence in humanity and humanity's being enveloped or clothed in God. She is able to do this because she sees all that is and all that will be having its being through the love of God. The vision came immediately "in a point," but the meaning came only gradually: "And from the time that it was revealed, I desired many times to know in what was our Lord's meaning. And fifteen years after and more, I was answered in spiritual understanding, and it was said: What, do you wish to know your Lord's meaning in this thing? Know it well, love was his meaning. Who reveals it to you? Love. What did he reveal to you? Love. Why does he reveal it to you? For love. Remain in this, and you will know more of the same. But you will never know different, without end. So I was taught that love is our Lord's meaning."

Julian's tellings of her experience reflect a disciplined movement from experience to concept and communication. The short version of her showings appears immediate and involves what some have interpreted as an almost random juxtaposition of images. But the immediacy of this version implies a close, largely unreflective, connection with experience. That experience is dominated by proximity to death, clinically described but also passionately experienced when Julian holds the whole universe in the palm of her hand. It is also dominated by the paradox of sin and pain in a world sustained by God's love: she experiences the assurance that all manner of things will be well as a conundrum, not an answer. Both proximity to death and the paradox of sin and pain are dominated by the experience of God's love, but it is only after long reflection that she is able to put that experience into words with which she is satisfied.

The close, largely unreflective, connection with experience of the short version contrasted with the reflective distillation of the experience into words with which Julian is satisfied in the long version is indicative of a movement similar to Piaget's movement from action to concept.

We have to assume that both versions were constructed within a formal operational context. But we can also safely assume that the experience both versions describe is rooted, as Julian herself suggests, in her own history and in her historical context. What begins as a sickness—understood in terms wholly consistent with her time—becomes an encounter with God. That the sickness should take such a form is not entirely a matter of Julian's free choice—nor is her earlier prayer for the sickness. That prayer is itself a reflection of ambivalence toward embodiment, an ambivalence that is firmly rooted in the experience of the medieval church and particularly of women in the medieval church. Her prayer for a sickness unto death almost certainly reflects a culturally imposed rejection of embodiment consistent with the experience of saints and martyrs with whom she was familiar. Her experience is rooted in, but not limited to, that cultural imposition. This takes us beyond both the arbitrary choosing and the cultural imposition of stories.

The construction of identity is both a cultural (or social) and an individual (or psychological) process. This process is connected with both story and vision, but it is grounded in experience. In Julian's case, the construction of identity included embracing humanity, and, in the embrace, comprehending experience. It also included the showing (or telling) of experience. That sequence—experience, comprehension, communication—is consistent with Piaget's understanding of progression from sensory-motor activity through concrete to formal operations. It is also consistent with the understanding of that progression as a decentering in which identity is constructed in relationship.

Julian's experience provides a basis on which to construct a world and reconstruct God. Both constructions are essential elements in the construction of her self. That is precisely the point. For Julian, a relinquishing of power, an emptying of self, makes it possible for her to stand in relation to both God and the world. To speak of relinquishing power and emptying self in Julian's case may seem misleading. Given the culturally imposed powerlessness of women in her time, it would appear that she had no power to relinquish. But, again, that is precisely the point: power and self were both constructed in relationship. Julian's showings suggest that power is not so much something one possesses as it is the experience of being enveloped in love. That in turn is experienced as the embrace (or enveloping) of humanity which she most characteristically identifies with courtesy. "In love," she said, "is gentle courtesy."

Julian's vision provides a model of spiritual development in which seeking God involves finding oneself and finding the world—or, more properly, constructing one's self and one's world. T. S. Eliot not only quoted Julian in "Little Gidding," but also pictured the journey she describes:

Sin is Behovely, but
All shall be well, and
All manner of things shall be well . . .

What we call the beginning is often the end
And to make an end is to make a beginning.
The end is where we start from . . .

We shall not cease from exploration
And the end of all our exploring
Will be to arrive where we started
And know the place for the first time.

We will know the place for the first time because we will for the first time have made it.

❡Revising and expanding the definition with which James works, the point is not that the mystic is immobile or inactive but that his or her will is suspended in a transformative experience of the whole. In this particular place at this particular time, everything changes. The experience is unitive in that distinctions (inside/outside, for example) are suspended. It is an experience of knowing (and because it is a *knowing* not a *known*, it is an act) that is beyond words. It is an act with no subject that can be communicated only indirectly: what you can say is not it. It is what you cannot say. Mysticism is not a turn away from language, but a turn to language that attends to silence, intent on communicating what can be known no place else. This is a broadening of language to include what is not said.

If god is that in which we place our trust, the language of every time and place is theological in that it shows what is trusted in that time and place—in what is said, in what is not said, and in what cannot be said. Language always reveals and conceals—so what is said and what is not are equally products of what language does, particularly what one chooses to say and what one chooses not to say—as well as what one cannot say (or what one believes, for whatever reason, cannot be said). Knowing is the issue, and this is a matter of what we usually call science. What Bergson calls dynamic religion is experimental to the core.

Mystical thinking fascinates me because I think we often stumble in our attempts both to interpret and to change the world because we proceed as though the structure of human thinking and its connection with human action were narrative or logical. That is so nearly accurate as to be especially tempting. But I believe mystical thinking, broadly conceived, reveals a lyrical structure that proceeds synthetically via structures of the whole (to use Piagetian language again) rather than analytically in a linear asynchronous fashion. Human thinking, I am convinced, is more akin to music (broadly conceived to include lyric poetry) than to logic. Julian's *Showings* are exemplary in this regard—but I turn briefly now to a series of lyric poets in the Julian tradition for further insight.

Anglican spirituality (as Urban Holmes notes) is Augustinian (and this makes room for both Luther and Calvin)—but it is also Julian (as Holmes also notes) and Platonist via Plotinus and Origen. While Holmes flatly asserts that John Donne and the metaphysical poets are not mystics, I think Ralph Vaughan Williams was more nearly correct when he took up four of George Herbert's poems for his "Five Mystical Songs." If one is keen to highlight the extent to which Donne turns from a medieval toward a "modern" worldview, disentangling him from a category thoroughly identified with the medieval makes sense. But I find the continuity equally compelling, and I take it as an indication of how long the arc of that turn is—tracing its beginning back at least to Augustine (and probably Origen) through Julian and Wycliffe to the broad church authors of *Essays and Reviews*, F. D. Maurice and other founders of Christian Socialism, and Ralph Vaughan Williams. Approaching the question of god in an heretically (but I think consistently) Lutheran way, there is no "super" natural. With the incarnation, god disappears into humanity (and this is consistent also with the development that culminates in rabbinic Judaism). In a larger historical perspective, it is consistent with Aquinas to collapse "god" into language. Theology is language about god, and god is a concept (as John Lennon said) by which we measure our pain.

In his "Litany," Donne gathers twenty-seven almost (but not quite) Spenserian stanzas, 3^2 lines gathered into a poem of 3^3 stanzas, with a rhyme scheme throughout of ababcdcdd. The sequence begins with the sequence of the traditional litany that is also the sequence often employed in the writing of systematic theologies: Father, Son, Holy Spirit, Trinity (the fourth encompassing the first three). The sequence continues in a manner that suggests at least a glance toward Donne's Jesuit roots: Mary, angels, patriarchs, prophets, apostles, martyrs, confessors, virgins, and doctors. The structure, though not perfectly consistent in this regard, would work quite well in public worship with the first four lines being a call to which the next five respond.

Reading through the sequence, the first, addressed to the Father, depicts a creation in which we are for heaven and all else is for us. Note that the invocation is that I might rise from death *before* I am dead. There is a hierarchy in space that is collapsed by a conception of time that (as in Julian) emphasizes presence rather than a linear narrative structure in which one thing follows (and perhaps leads to) another. The second, addressed to the Son, asserts that sin and death were not *made*. There is a repetition of the crucifixion (again suggesting a structure of time that emphasizes presence) with *my* heart as the cross. The heart is drowned in blood, slain by the passion of the son of god. The third, which turns to the Holy Spirit, depicts the human being as a mud temple washed by fire. Fire it up, Donne prays; let fire, sacrifice, priest, and altar be the same. This could refer back to "intend"—meaning, here, to intensify. But it could also collapse them into one. The latter is consistent with the unitive turn of mysticism and, with the emphasis on presence, moves toward god being the agent of all action. The fourth stanza, which takes up the Trinity, is a comment on human rationality. Philosophy chokes on the trinity, while faith feeds on it. The invocation here is that I might be composed of power, love, and knowledge in the same way the trinity is composed.

The fifth stanza is a characteristically Anglican approach to Mary. Donne sees it as acceptable to Catholics but not offensive to Calvinists (though one suspects many Calvinists, then and now, would disagree). The "strange heaven" of Mary's womb is an interesting way to think about incarnation. The one "claim for innocence" that "disseized" sin is an image of *theopoiein*.

The stanzas following, six through fourteen, are a prayer for humility in reason—and so turn from the Godhead to humanity by way of Mary. This life is our childhood (our "nonage"). We are wards of the angels, who are natives of heaven while we will be only naturalized citizens. The invocation here is for actions worthy of sight though they are blind to how they see. The "eagle-sighted" prophets are cited as "heavenly poets," the eyes of the Church; but stanza nine reminds us not to speak as though we speak for God. Stanzas thirteen and fourteen remind us to honor the doctors of the church as stars but not to confuse them with the sun and asks that we be delivered from trusting in prayers. Stanzas fourteen through twenty-two are prayers for deliverance that follow the traditional form of the litany. All pray that we be delivered from idolatry.

And then the litany turns toward a statement of divine agency ("thou in us dost pray") that ends with an explicitly Julian spirituality: "As sin is nothing, let it nothing be."

The holy sonnet "I am a little world..." depicts the "I" as a microcosm, which, like the larger world, is composed of elements and "an angelic sprite"—an image that evokes

Descartes. Note that both parts die because sin has betrayed them to night. The space (in lines 1-4) is between light and night, and it seems that we can turn either way in it. After a reference (apparently) to the *Sidereus Nuncius* of Galileo, Donne builds in a series of biblical references that evoke a new flood and (in lines 9-10) the fire that was promised "next time." The final four lines contrast two kinds of fire—one (the fire of lust and envy) turned away from, the other (the fire of zeal) turned toward the light.

In his "Anatomy of the World," Donne connects a single death, a particular occasion, with the sickness of the world. By calling this an anatomy, he suggests that the world has already died, a point that he makes explicit by line 60. Donne begins by asking who is sure s/he has a soul. He connects knowledge of the soul with action and (line 6) distinguishes between having an "inmate soul" and having a soul of one's own. Having a soul (rather than simply containing one) depends on action turned toward good.

This is an interesting comment in terms of one of the central theological controversies of the time, the nature of human work. There is a potentially Calvinist flavor in this approach to action, in that one may be inclined to do good work to demonstrate one's election. But Donne seems to take a different turn, as suggested by his depiction of the incarnation (lines 167-170) as God coming down to humankind until humankind comes up to God. The image is characteristically Julian and characteristically Anglican. In the incarnation, God lifts earth to heaven by bending heaven to earth. That these seemingly opposite movements are seen as one movement is critical. When Donne writes "'Tis all in pieces, all coherence gone; / All just supply, and all relation: / Prince, subject, father, son, are things forgot, / For every man alone thinks he hath got /

To be a phoenix, and that there can be / None of that kind, of which he is, but he," he describes the world's condition now—but he also affirms, in the middle of that condition, that there is no *man alone*. He does this most clearly in the meditations that follow his own near death experience when he says "No man is an island..." Every death diminishes the whole of humankind, and that justifies taking the "anatomy" of a particular death as an anatomy of the whole world. It also underwrites a Socratic attitude toward death in which life is a disease, and death is the cure. Donne's spin on this is that the body is the soul's womb, death the midwife. When the body dies, the soul is born. But that requires a reorientation of time, more linear than is characteristic of Donne. The soul is present from the beginning in the beginning of the poem. The question is whether it is simply an "inmate" of the body or an integral part of the person composed of body (elements, as noted earlier) and soul (the angelic sprite). Donne's answer leans toward the idea of the soul as the form of the body, and this is cast in terms of the poem—his work: "Vouchsafe to call to mind, that God did make / A last, and lasting'st piece, a song. He spake / To Moses, to deliver unto all, / That song: because he knew they would let fall / The Law, the prophets, and the history, / But keep the song still in their memory."

Donne's "Hymn to God the Father" is addressed to the first person of the Trinity. The first question is whether the Father will forgive original sin, which is my sin, though it were from before. The second is whether the Father will forgive the sins the poet has "run through" although he deplores them. Now, to whom are the last two lines addressed? Do they mean that, when the Father is done he has not Donne, who is not through sinning? And what of making More the source of not having here? Is it a comment on works? What you do you have not done—in which case it would presumably not apply to God, certainly not to the whole trinity. In the second stanza, there is a third question—the sin by which I have led others to sin—and a fourth, the lifetime of sin. The third stanza names a sin of fear, not fear of death but fear of dying apart from God, which is the moment of turning to the Son/sun, asking the Father to swear that the sun will go on shining. that casts out fear, which is what perfect love does. So the movement of the poem is to a paradoxical trinity in which a loss is connected with union with the divine—*in thy light we see light*, a trinitarian theology that is a comment on how we know.

The opening two lines (the first sentence) of "To Sir Henry Wotten" comment on an incarnational theology important to the understanding of presence. It highlights the importance of letters in the 17th century, which, we should bear in mind, means that century has much in common with ours by way of the value it places on virtual dimensions of a relationship: "Sir, more than kisses, letters mingle souls; / For, thus friends absent speak...." The sequence of sin (from angels to men, with "beasts" excluded) is interesting. Lines 49 and following anticipate some of Deleuze's philosophy of nomadism. This is presented partly as an antidote to schism.

In "Good Friday, 1613, Riding Westward," the soul is the intelligence that moves, the sphere in which devotion is. Imagining this sphere in a Ptolemaic universe, the outer spheres affect its motion—*by others hurried every day* it forgets its natural form and is whirled by *pleasure or business*. The soul's form bends eastward—toward the sunrise but also toward Jerusalem and the cross—but the poet rides westward. Christ rising and falling on the cross is the light of the world—without this, sin would have *benighted all*. It is a matter of turning—toward God or toward self. Donne speaks of the death of God as the antidote for sin's darkness. Christ's blood is the seal of all our souls. The Marian devotion is not surprising in an Anglican context. In the ending—restore my image so you will recognize me, and I will turn to face you—the emphasis is on turning (as a human act) and restoration (as God's act). This is consistent with Julian's universalism, and it is at least an implicit embrace of Origen's *apokatastasis*—not in the sense of a restoration to an Edenic age but in the sense of love (and, more fully, justice and mercy embracing in love) as the fundamental structure of the universe: god is love, and love is all there is.

All of this may be called into question by reference to Donne's biography as a tortured soul, and this is sometimes done in conjunction with an Augustinian reading. Donne's autobiographical construction of himself follows closely the pattern Augustine established, in which the later life—after conversion—is sharply distinguished from the earlier. Both may also be contrasted with Julian, who appears to be far more at ease with the embrace of love from the beginning.

But this is misleading in all three cases. It neglects the fact that Augustine's *Confessions* is an autobiographical reconstruction with a homiletic (and rhetorical) intention. But there is arguably one self that emerges in the whole, and that self is (as Augustine would be the first to acknowledge) altogether *coram deo*. It neglects the fact that we have only two snapshots of Julian, the second of which is probably more accurately depicted as a carefully composed portrait. It is likely that if we had more detail of the life she lived before, between, and after these glimpses, we would see more of the struggle and the conversion that we see in Augustine and in Donne. That we don't see it is evidence of Julian's Augustinian emphasis on the *presence* of God (from beginning to end) more than on a process of conversion in which the new simply succeeds the old. The new makes *all* things new, and the whole is transformed, beginning to end, in the presence of God. That is a characterization of the structure of time (in which, as Augustine described it, there is not past, present, and future but rather a present of things past, a present of things present, and a present of things future). Julian embraces this fully and makes it also a characterization of space in which all is the presence of god. There is no place where god is not.

With Donne, we return to a body of evidence that includes a long conversion and a long struggle—often characterized as reluctance to enter the priesthood overcome only when that appeared to be the only option left. But I suggest that what we see is a Julian embrace of the whole in which the "profane" poems written by the young Donne are as sacramental as the sermons he preached up to the end of his life. There is no place where god is not, no thing so small as to be insignificant. A flea is as fitting a subject for poetry as the whole world, and a single death can serve as the body in an autopsy of the whole world. That it is an autopsy, I repeat, is an indication that the world is already dead. So it is not a matter of being saved from "this" world to eternal life in an "other" world. There is one living world, and we are in it, body and soul.

The question is how to open eyes to that reality. It is, as is so often the case in mystical experience, a matter of seeing.

VI

¶The first problem entering a conversation at the intersection of religion and ethics is that, in any particular instance of the conversation, some participants will have no *idea* of one or the other—or of either, though all *practice, will practice, and will have practiced* one or both at one time or another. A second problem is that, in any particular instance, some participants will have an idea of one or the other or both so entrenched that all will go without saying and none will be open to question in practice. A third problem is that, as the idea of poetry is prose, the idea of religion is ethics. An idea of poetry is no poem; attending to the idea turns poetry to prose. And an idea of religion (even a religious one) is no religion. When religious practice turns to its *idea*, it turns to ethics.

This statement of these problems gestures toward Kierkegaard's understanding of the relationship between the ethical and the religious—and the relationship of both to the aesthetic. In time, the aesthetic, which is *immediate*, is first. It may be followed by the ethical, which is *mediate*. That, in turn, may be followed by the religious, which is *immediate* again. Passing through the ethical is the difference between *immediate* and immediate *again*, and, because that difference makes a difference to both religion and ethics, it affects the intersection.

Before attending to the difference, note that immediacy is a mark of the aesthetic that marks the religious in time: immediacy is aesthetic, not ethical, because there is no time in it (and hence no place) for ethical deliberation. Given time, ethics may take place. Because the religious returns to immediacy (meaning that the religious is always a *return*), it leaves no place in practice for ethics; and that makes it aesthetic. The aesthetic envelops the ethical; it is *religious* on its leading edge.

That *again* is a possibility (both in the sense of repetition—as in Kierkegaard—and return—as in Nietzsche) makes all the difference. The ethical follows the aesthetic;

it does not supersede it. And the religious follows both but supersedes neither. That *again* is possible, however, means that, once one has entered the religious, one can enter either the ethical or the aesthetic or both *after* the religious. But passing through the ethical—coming or going—is always the difference between the religious and the aesthetic—or, as suggested in passing earlier, between two aesthetics. (What Paul Ricoeur, perhaps, had in mind, in his distinction between a first and a second naiveté.)

While the ethical is, as Kierkegaard put it, universal, it is also (and perhaps more properly) communicative, because it is *mediate*. It is where reflection and communication take place, and it depends on categories that can be shared as well as rules that can be obeyed or broken. The aesthetic *resists* categories (there is no accounting for taste), and this accounts for the tension on both boundaries between the aesthetic and the ethical. The tension, as Kierkegaard noted, is *interesting*—and interest is a key concept for border crossing. The interesting moves us when we encounter a border and may move us across it; being *moved* may be the best indicator that we have reached a border worth crossing. Remember Kierkegaard's insistence that faith is a passion, not an action: before we move, we are *moved*. *Being moved demands our attention.*

VII

¶ Kierkegaard's interest in border categories derives at least in part from his recognition that reason alone does not move human beings to do the right thing and cannot adequately account for the wrong things we do: rational beings acting rationally are perfectly capable of making cities that are neither good nor beautiful—and, therefore, though rational, are not true. Herbert Marcuse and other critical theorists developed this idea at length in analyses of destructive systems each piece of which could pass rational scrutiny but, that taken all together, behave as if out of their minds. The strategists of United States nuclear policy during the Cold War had humor enough to call their system of deterrence MAD. Naming a system, like naming a demon, is an important step in exorcising it—and it is worth noting that, in an exorcism, the step depends on knowing the name by which the demon names itself. But, beyond naming, the question is how to *turn it*— and Kierkegaard, like his contemporary Marx, saw this as a task that might lead philosophy beyond itself.

Driving philosophy out of its mind might prove critical to critical reflection inside a system that is mad. That, of course, is a dangerous game: a philosopher driven out of his or her mind may be sidelined as a lunatic. (Nietzsche and Elfriede Jelinek both have something to say about that.) But out of mind may also mean into body—into what moves us, what moves when we move, and that is a critical step if interpretation is to be connected with change. Calling a mad system mad does not in and of itself change behavior that makes it so. As Joseph Heller reminded us, naming the madness of a mad system may simply feed the rational mechanisms by which the system is maintained: to recognize it as mad is the most rational thing one can do, an assurance that policy is in the hands of policy makers and critics who can be counted upon to be reasonable. But *interest* is something else, powering the very turns a system must contain if it is to avoid flying off in all directions.

There are familiar contexts in which *be reasonable* is equivalent to *contain yourself*—and a perfectly rational system of containment is most perfectly self sustaining when that is precisely what happens (an important point of convergence between "Western" and Confucian philosophy that is of interest to those seeking to understand mechanisms of social control by which political systems are sustained across time). Interest, though, always threatens to spill out of the containers designed to keep it in line. So Kierkegaard turns to instances in which characters cannot contain themselves and, as a result, cannot explain themselves. Abraham, moved to murder his son, was condemned to silence. He did not choose it; if he was prepared to murder his son, there were no words for it. And, as Kierkegaard saw it, this moved him outside the realm of the ethical—outside ordinary action motivated by interests within the constraints of a system that contained him. He could not contain himself. The system could not contain him. And that is *interesting*. It is interesting particularly because it unleashes a power that threatens to shatter the system itself. If Abraham cannot be contained, there is a real danger that no one can. And in that danger hope also lies.

All of this is preliminary—pointing to the power of interest on edges of containment, possibilities of not being contained. Pointing to power recalls Foucault's observation that power comes from everywhere (not that power is everything) and highlights the extent to which processes of containment depend on distinctions among centers, while challenges to containment depend on acting from centers that are not *authorized*. It is a question of legitimacy that turns on balances of power often mediated by language and other symbol systems: power is contained by being balanced and channeled. When power overflows its channels, balance is threatened. And unbalanced individuals are dealt with in predictable ways, by being institutionalized—as citizens, as criminals, as saints, as lunatics—or by being eliminated—executed or rendered invisible.

The first category, *citizens*, is of particular interest because it is the ordinary condition of balance in which people who play by the rules find themselves. It is often understood as a balancing act, finding one's feet in an interplay of powers that include (but are not limited to) one's own—and it is in this context that both ethical and legal behavior are often understood in terms of competing interests, as evidenced by the place of self interest in everyday conversation and conflict of interest in ethical judgments and explanations of particular behaviors. Had Abraham consulted his attorney, he would likely have been advised to recuse himself from this assignment because of a conflict of interest concerning his son (and his relationship to the boy's mother, as well as the earlier promise of a gift from the person responsible for assigning the task). If God wanted the boy sacrificed, he would have been well advised to assign the task to someone undeterred by such conflicts. And, though God is presumably someone else's client, assigning the task to someone who has been promised a gift not only creates a conflict of interest for Abraham but also creates the appearance of impropriety on God's part. There are problems all around, and this means of executing the task is not likely to contribute to the stability of the organization.

Ordinary discourse about ordinary behavior, often involving extraordinary tasks, is ordinarily cast in terms of interest. Standard accounts assume that *self* interest is a given, while the interests of *others* are suspect. More often than not (especially in economic and sometimes legal theory) rational behavior is understood to be behavior that is consistent with the self interest of the agent. "Rational choice" theory in economics contends that such behavior, consistently pursued, will result in a "rational" social structure. Controversy often takes the form of different understandings of the extent to which the social structure ought to intervene consciously (and can intervene consciously) to constrain behavior. Centralized planning is generally thought to have been discredited by the failure of command economies; but there are varying degrees of faith in the ability of emergent structures to self-correct in rational ways—and differences of opinion about whether what is believed true of economic systems applies directly to other social systems.

What I find intriguing is that self interest, understood as a given, is acceptable within limits that legal theorists and courts struggle to define on a case by case basis. Generally speaking, while it is assumed that rational agents act in ways that are consistent with their own self interest, when self interest is judged to have crossed a line into self enrichment—especially in fiduciary relationships—it is considered (at least) ethically questionable and (possibly) illegal. In fiduciary relationships, the legal approach seems to be predicated on the need to protect the interests of others (which the fiduciary is obligated to pursue) from self interest (which the fiduciary, being human, will *naturally* pursue). In conflict of interest cases, the legal practice, it seems, is to place limits on those interests assumed to be "natural" in order to protect *legal* interests that are not. Ethically, that action is best that is least motivated by "natural" inclinations. The law, it seems, is supposed to function in such a way as to insure that action is undertaken on the basis of legal/contractual obligations among strangers. That is interesting for what it says about strangers as well as what it says about the sources of our obligations. The emphasis is on the legal/contractual obligation, not the stranger. And ties of family, friendship, passion are all viewed as forces to be held in check.

What most troubled Kierkegaard about the binding of Isaac was the ease with which such a text of terror could be bound within a legal tradition. Whether the emphasis is on Abraham's willingness to do whatever he believed God commanded or on Ishmael's willingness to submit to whatever his father believed God commanded, this terror is too much to contain. Even if the emphasis is on God's repenting of the command just in time to save Isaac (or Ishmael) from the knife, the terror is beyond words. How can Isaac (or Ishmael) and Abraham ever face one another again without the glint of the knife flashing in the corner of the eye?

The ethical is suspended in the terror of the present moment. (Kierkegaard called the suspension "teleological," but I think we are best served by suspending the *telos* as well). That turns us back to the stranger and, more generally, to the other we know with varying degrees of familiarity. The ethical is essentially contractual—a legal arrangement rationally executed at least in part so we know what we can expect and what we can do if the contract is, unexpectedly, violated. The unexpected becomes essential as we move to the borders of the ethical, and the question is how we are to act when we cannot know what to expect. The other, especially the stranger, defies expectation and, merely by being present, constitutes an obligation. Obligation arises, perhaps, from the *fact* of a limit (which informs Derrida's understanding of death as gift). Such limits, in fact, are critical to the formation of *selves* without which *self* interest is not possible. Obligation precedes self interest—and is, in turn, preceded by the being present of the stranger—oneself as another, to an other, to one's self as an other.

The most wholly other most wholly demands response. Response, not rule, is the basis of obligation, which grows out of an absolute demand to welcome the stranger. The ethical, as contractual relationship, is not temporarily suspended by the demand of the wholly other. It is temporarily imposed when the other is not acknowledged as being there. Rules by which interest is held in check contain strangeness by imposing predictability. The appearance of the stranger defies predictability and takes us back to where *we* begin—in the encounter of one self with an other. The "we" Agnes Heller wrote, "is that through which I am." Yes. And we is I to I, a circle out of which systems of obligation may be formed.

The point is not to build legal systems that, by holding interests in check, enable contractual agreements among strangers. It is to mobilize interest as a means by which to turn to strangers, to turn strangers to guests, to make us inclined to give our lives for friends rather than to take the lives of others we love in the name of arbitrary gods. If the demand to sacrifice our children is a test, we pass it when we say no. And so, for ethics and religion, what gives us pause is as critical as what moves us.

VIII

¶ Samuel Taylor Coleridge locates the certainty of our knowledge in affirmation of the immediate that dwells in every person (though consciousness of it does not). Language, the medium of ordinary communication, plays off the surfaces that constitute matter—like smoke and mirrors or shadows on the inside surface of a cave. (Matter, he says, has no *inward*.) The medium of the depth, however, is freedom. We have, he says, "imprisoned our own conceptions by the lines, which we have drawn, in order to exclude the conceptions of others." As a result, we live not so much in a cave as in a labyrinth of closets of our own making.

Responding to this, he offers a variation on Hegel's negation of the negation. "I find," he says, "that most sects are reasonable in a good part of what they advance—but not in what they deny." This is a basis on which to elaborate grammars, logics, and rhetorics of freedom—necessary if freedom is to be a medium of communication in the "spiritual" world analogous to language as a medium of communication in the "material" one. Because we live in a "material" world oriented toward a "spiritual" one, we live in necessity toward freedom. In Coleridge's critical theory, active imagination forms poetry out of the material—language—in which it works, toward the medium—freedom—in which it lives.

He collapses epistemological and ontological questions in his articulation of transcendental philosophy, folding ethical questions into the mix as well. The postulate of philosophy, the ground from which it begins, he says, is "the heaven-descended know thyself," an injunction that is simultaneously practical and speculative: philosophy is not only a science of reason or understanding (an epistemology), not only a science of morals (an ethic), but also a science of being (an ontology). Its primary ground cannot be either merely speculative or merely practical; it must be both at the same time. Knowledge rests on "the coincidence of an object with a subject."

Coleridge calls the objective *Nature*, the subjective *intelligence*. Intelligence is representative, Nature represented. Knowledge is an act that consists in "a reciprocal concurrence of both," in which the two are so instantly united that one cannot determine which takes priority. Either the objective is taken as first and we have to account for the coincidence of the subjective, or the subjective is taken as first and we have to account for the coincidence of the objective. These are equally important poles of fundamental science. In both cases, we are confronted with a union of opposites in which Nature is infused with intelligence and intelligence with Nature. Coleridge maintains that this is neither idealism nor materialism, but *realism*.

He maintains that to know is in its essence an active verb; that truth is either derivative or immediate; that the only immediate truth is an absolute identity of subject and object, of finite and infinite. That immediate truth or absolute identity—which Coleridge refers to as spirit, self, or self-consciousness—is not a kind of being but a kind of knowing. On the basis of this immediate truth that is a kind of knowing, he distinguishes *imagination* from *fancy* and primary imagination from secondary. Primary imagination is "the living Power and prime Agent of all human Perception," a repetition of the eternal act of creation. Secondary imagination is an echo, differing from primary imagination only in degree: it dissolves in order to recreate. Both varieties of imagination differ from objects in that they are active, while objects are fixed. Objects live to the extent that they are infused with vital imagination. Fancy is a mode of memory that "must receive all its materials ready made from the law of association." Fancy lives in the spontaneous consciousness of the sensory world. It reflects passively, like a mirror—and it does not create. Imagination lives in the philosophical consciousness of the spiritual world. It reflects actively, recapitulating the creative act by breathing life into dead matter. Primary imagination is the soul of the world.

Early in *Biographia Literaria*, Coleridge defines *essential* poetry as that which we not only read with pleasure but *return to* with pleasure, and that which cannot be translated into other words of the same language without loss of significance. The image of return highlights the extent to which poetic genius consists in a continuously present undercurrent rather than a separate and transitory excitement. Keeping in mind the image of active imagination as the soul of the world, this is another way of pointing to the sustaining power of poetry as well as establishing the sustained attention of criticism: critical judgment rests not in reaction to accidental failures or shortcomings, but in careful exploration of qualities essential to the whole body of a poet's work. That Coleridge grounds both poetry and criticism in sustained attention to the essential qualities of a whole body of work is indicative of the close connection he saw between poetry and philosophy, between both and imagination. Poetic genius carries the feelings of childhood into the powers of adulthood, combining the child's sense of wonder with a lifetime of experience. Poetry and philosophy rescue universally accepted truths from impotence by continually making them new, digging beneath the surface to depths that are inexhaustible. This understanding grows out of conversation with William Wordsworth regarding two cardinal points of poetry: "the power of exciting the sympathy of the reader by a faithful adherence to the truth of nature, and the power of giving the interest of novelty by the modifying colors of imagination." These cardinal points are related to the distinction between fancy and imagination. A simple mirroring of the sensuous world (fancy) would quickly degenerate into banality, reproducing the world without transforming it. But, because imagination is active, it makes the world new.

Philosophical discussion proceeds by distinction, not division. The philosophical and poetic process of distinction combines active and passive dimensions in a serpentine movement. Truth is distinguished into its component parts, and the unity of these parts is conceptually restored. Just as a leap requires that one both defy gravity and submit to it, the process of philosophy requires both distinction and unity if it is not only to get off the ground but also return to it. A poem is composed of the same elements as a prose composition, but there is a difference in form as well as object—not what a particular piece of writing is *about* but the end toward which it is directed. Prose is characterized by having truth as its immediate end with pleasure as a possible secondary result. It is primarily concerned with knowing—understood particularly in terms of communication as transmission of information, only secondarily with feeling. But poetry is marked by its primary concern with pleasure. A poem is "that species of composition, which is opposed to works of science, by proposing for its *immediate* object pleasure, not truth; and from all other species (having *this* object in common with it) it is discriminated by proposing to itself such delight from the *whole*, as is compatible with a distinct gratification from each component *part*."

That pleasure is poetry's primary object does not diminish truth's importance. Nothing can *permanently* please if it does not "contain in itself the reason why it is so, and not otherwise." Attention must be sustained, not sporadic. If the form of a composition is detachable from its object, it is nothing more than a vehicle by which to get at the object—and one vehicle may serve this purpose as well as another, though none will serve it perfectly. If, however, composition and object are inextricably connected, neither object nor composition is expendable or exchangeable. Prose gestures toward truth, and it may carry us some way toward it; if so, it will impart pleasure. Poetry embodies truth in its form as well as its end. To the extent that it succeeds, pleasure is its end and its embodiment is truth. The distinction between poetry and prose, then, is not a distinction between poetry and philosophy. Because poetry is uniquely concerned with wholeness, it is the proper language of philosophy. Philosophical prose will necessarily be fragmentary and depend on poetry for both its composition and its comprehension.

A legitimate poem is one "the parts of which mutually support and explain each other; all in their proportion harmonizing with, and supporting the purpose and known influences of metrical arrangement." Harmony is a critical standard by which to judge the legitimacy of a composition: if it does not sing, it is not a poem. Which leads to the question of the poet. The poet "brings the whole soul...into activity," harmonizing discordant qualities by the power of imagination. The poet, in short, is an embodied poem.

In the discussion of common language that Coleridge and Wordsworth initiated with *Lyrical Ballads*, poetics and politics interpenetrate. An ideal polity, like an ideal poet, embodies poetry. Every part supports and explains every other; every part and every relation harmonizes with and supports the whole. Wordsworth maintained in his preface to *Lyrical Ballads* that language taken from real life is the proper diction for poetry and that this language actually constitutes natural human conversation. Coleridge offers three objections. First, the observation is applicable only in a limited class of poetry: it is true of some poems, but not all. Second, its application in this limited class is simply commonplace, not a subject for argument. And, third, it is at best useless and at worst harmful when applied as a rule. He does not object to the claim that the language of poetry is the language of real life, insisting, in fact, quite consistently that poetic language is the *most* real language, closest to the freedom he identifies as the medium of the spiritual world toward which our lives in the sensual world are turned. But the claim is sometimes interpreted to mean that poetry should be written in "rustic" or "vulgar" language. Where Wordsworth represents conversational speech, he recasts it in poetic form and so refines it. This, Coleridge argues, is precisely what poetry should do: seek not the commonest language but the greatest refinement of the common speech. The poet's task is the turning of soul in refinement of language. This is why the observation is a commonplace in the class of poetry where it applies: Wordsworth's experiments with common subjects and common speech are undeniably real language, but they are not simply transcriptions of common speech. Such transcription is one disastrous result of a mechanical application of Wordsworth's observation as a rule. Creativity is sacrificed, the poetry does not sing, and souls turn toward the sensuous rather than the spiritual world.

Coleridge outlines his method in a long note in the middle of an even longer comment on an aphorism in *Aids to Reflection*. The subject of the aphorism, from the Cambridge Platonist Robert Leighton, is redemption—more particularly the distance beyond nature's reach of a crucified Saviour. Here is a reality that extends far beyond the reach of understanding; but it is not, Coleridge insists, irrational. The distinction is critical. Where it is not properly drawn, we cannot hope to penetrate beyond surface phenomena. Drawing it is a matter of method. The method—which bears a family resemblance to Kant (and therefore Hegel and Marx), though it is not simply derivative—is built on a triadic structure derived from a Pythagorean understanding of the geometry of the line. A line may be drawn from a point midway between two extremes, indifferent with regard to the extremes, identifiable with either, identical to neither. Applied to logic, the extremes may be called *thesis* and *antithesis*. The midpoint, equally identifiable with either pole, Coleridge calls *mesothesis*. This mesothesis may be conceived as both thesis and antithesis, but not both at the same time: relative to the thesis, the mesothesis is equal to the antithesis; relative to the antithesis, it is equal to the thesis. The mesothesis does not bring thesis and antithesis together, but occupies (and defines) middle ground while it is pulled from moment to moment one way or the other. The third term in popular expositions of dialectic is *synthesis*, which, by bringing together thesis and antithesis, comprehends both. Coleridge maintains, however, that this convergence depends on a comprehensive *prothesis* present before thesis, antithesis, and mesothesis. He imagines the Pythagoreans rendering the constructions of pure mathematics applicable to philosophy by generating the line from a point which it does not contain—independent of the line, transcendent to its production. The assumption of this transcendent generative point is the prothesis. With its assumption in relation to the line, four relations of thought are expressed: prothesis, or *identity* of thesis and antithesis; thesis, or *position*; antithesis, or *opposition*; and mesothesis, or *indifference*. Synthesis adds *composition*. Prothesis, thesis, antithesis, mesothesis, and synthesis together make up a *noetic pentad* which describes the rhythm of distinction and comprehension characteristic of reason: below (or behind) distinction lies the unity of prothesis, above (or beyond) it lies the unity of synthesis. Coleridge connects analytic and synthetic, practical and pure, reason in what he calls "the five most general forms or preconceptions of constructive logic."

With this, Coleridge returns to the *Idea*, which is neither an impression on the senses or a mere abstraction from sensory data. Beginning with the absolutely real as prothesis, the subjectively real as thesis, and the objectively real as antithesis, he identifies *Idea* as mesothesis: conceived as in the subject, it is an object; conceived as in the object, it is a subject. This is the two step serpentine movement of active imagination described in *Biographia Literaria*. And it is related to the distinction between understanding and reason, arguably the most important contribution of *Aids to Reflection*. Coleridge describes the difference between reason and understanding as a difference *in kind*, and he outlines it most explicitly in the section of *Aids to Reflection* devoted to "spiritual religion indeed." The outline follows a comment on another aphorism from Leighton: "Faith elevates the soul not only above sense and sensible things, but above reason itself. As reason corrects the errors which sense might occasion, so supernatural faith corrects the errors of natural reason judging according to sense." Coleridge laments a pervasive tendency in British thought to include two faculties under the one heading of "reason," which, under the influence of Locke, is always derivative from sensation and opposite to faith. In order to properly distinguish these faculties, he proposes a consistent application of two terms—reason and understanding. Understanding is discursive, derivative, and reflective. Reason is fixed, substantial, and contemplative. Understanding is "the faculty by which we reflect and generalize." He describes understanding as a three step process relative to (but only partly dependent on) sensation: attention, abstraction, and generalization. The first step is passive: our attention is appropriated; the second is active: we attend selectively; the third is comparative and synthetic. As a whole, the function (or end) of the understanding is generalization of sensory data in the construction of names. It is "a faculty judging according to sense," but it is also an active faculty that constructs categories. Reason, on the other hand, is "the source of necessary and universal principles, according to which the notices of the senses are either affirmed or denied and the power by which we are enabled to draw from particular and contingent appearances universal and necessary conclusions." Understanding is dependent on and posterior to sensation, while reason is independent and anterior.

Coleridge objects to the passivity and determinism of Lockean *reason*, not so much a term as a confusion that, because it conflates two faculties that differ in kind, is not even half right. The conflation of faculties results in a language of necessity that undermines both freedom and communication. Neither understanding nor reason is simply passive. Both proceed by the serpentine rhythm of action and passion described in *Biographia Literaria* with reference to imagination. Understanding abstracts on the basis of both reason and sensation; resting on wholes, it weaves parts together. Reason is the whole by which understanding operates on sensation. This is partly a matter of the direction, partly a matter of the operation of thought: in Leighton's aphorism, reason corrects sensation, faith corrects reason, and our soul is lifted above both. From sensation through reason to transcendence, the soul is a butterfly the world sends fluttering on its way. But Coleridge looks for *ground*: from transcendent reason through sensation and understanding toward comprehension and communication, the soul, grounded in the world, grounds the world in God.

IX

¶ Soul grounded in the world that grounds the world in God calls to mind how Kierkegaard described "the condition of the self when despair is completely eradicated" in *The Sickness Unto Death*: "by relating itself to its own self and by willing to be itself the self is grounded transparently in the Power which posited it." Being grounded transparently marks a return to immediacy that echoes

Coleridge's description of poetic genius as carrying the "feelings of childhood into the powers of adulthood, combining the child's sense of wonder with a lifetime of experience"—grounded, yes; but carried away. And that image carries us to another English poet often identified with the beginning of the "Romantic" movement, even more often associated with being *touched* and *seeing things*, William Blake.

Encountering Blake's work means encountering vision whole—not "a vision" reported by an observer, but the act itself, an embodied refutation of Locke's depiction of the mind of the child as a blank slate. His work, which demonstrates a mind engaged in a world of its making, is an invitation to engage all the senses in the perpetual birthing of a world always new. One can't simply read Blake with transparent eyes through which an author is expected to engrave fixed truths on a blank mind. One must engage him, eyes first, then ears—not because sight takes precedence over sound but because vision contains sound as well as sight, both tactile. Vision is an experience of the whole body, an interplay of sight, sound, taste, smell that *touches* us. In the touch, meaning is made. Blake, as many of his friends and acquaintances suspected, was touched; and we cannot encounter him without being touched as well.

Blake reclaimed a tradition of English lyric that is more Spenser than Milton, though it is something of both; and it is Biblical to the core. But he did it in an urban context where he listened for the music of the city with ears trained by a pastoral tradition to hear shepherd's songs. When Blake heard the chimney sweep, he recognized the music of Albion, a music he could not disconnect from his vision of a new Jerusalem. And he could not convey a vision of a city of music that reached back through the bleak landscape of late eighteenth and early nineteenth century London to an essentially pastoral epic tradition in words alone. He needed images. He needed to sing them as the folk did on the streets of London. And he needed to share a vision—a poetry of the eyes as well as the ears. This is what led him to the "illuminated books" that began with *Songs of Innocence* and evolved into *Songs of Innocence and of Experience Shewing the Two Contrary States of the Human Soul*. Calling the books "illuminated" recalls the monastic tradition of adding images to the words of manuscripts prepared by hand, but it also directs our attention to the light that is so important to Blake's engravings, which often seem to glow. Blake did not add images to words. He composed poetry of both and used it to illuminate a soul formed in the tension of two states, not a progression from one state to another.

The method by which he composed poetry of words and images was suggested in a vision by his dead brother Robert and is illustrated in the making of the *Songs*. Images and words were etched onto a copper plate used to print the pages of the book which were later colored by hand. This had the practical effect of reducing costs: and, because what would have been accomplished in two steps could in this way be accomplished in one, words and images were integrated into the same act. In order to accomplish the etching process in one step, Blake had to master the art of mirror writing; so he became expert in writing in reverse, an interesting exercise for an artist convinced that our humanity is composed of contraries. But he also worked by burning away surfaces that were not essential to the words and images of the book—a reversal of Locke's blank slate. Rather than writing on an empty tablet, he developed a process by which to expose new words and images on one that was full.

While the book took shape from 1788 to 1793, the printing process evolved. *Songs of Innocence* was printed then colored by hand with transparent watercolors—a watercolor wash over a monochrome print. *Songs of Experience*, first printed five years later, was color printed with opaque pigments. In both cases, the etching process itself involved painting with acid-resistant varnish on copper plate—marking what was to be saved from the corrosive influence of the acid into which the plate was plunged. For *Songs of Innocence*, monochrome prints were made from the plates, then colored with transparent wash. For *Songs of Experience*, opaque pigment was applied directly to the plates, resulting in more richly colored, denser prints. As Blake saw it, the watercolor wash was more like painting with light than with pigment. For the viewer, the experience of *Innocence* is that of seeing light reflected off a ground through transparent color. *Experience* is the reflection of light off the opaque pigment itself. And there is metaphysical significance to this. For Blake, vision is entangled with penetration to depths that are not fully exposed under layers of experience. One effect of experience is a layering that renders depths less accessible to ordinary vision: experience is never transparent. The interplay of the paired poems in this collection (most famously, perhaps, "The Lamb" and "The Tyger") is intended to recover depths more immediately accessible to childhood's "innocent" eyes than to the "experienced" eyes of adulthood. There is a progression in the poems—not from innocence to experience, but from unorganized to organized innocence, with the contrary states of innocence and experience maintaining tension throughout. (Recall the description of the movement from immediate through mediate to immediate *again*. Kierkegaard's "ethical" parallels Blake's "experience," and the difference between the two *immedi-*

ates is akin to that between unorganized and organized innocence.) In human existence, innocence is never pure, and experience does not outgrow it. Vision always takes place in between—and that it takes place in between is highlighted by the making of the book: in the interplay of word and image in *Songs of Innocence*, painted with light in watercolor wash; in the pairing of poems and the tension between the translucent images of *Innocence* and the opaque color-printed images of *Experience*; in the creation of the images of *Experience* on the pages of a sketchbook begun by Blake's brother Robert; and in the open-ended form of the book itself, which was produced not as a bound and fixed object but as a collection of prints ready to be bound at the point of sale.

Two of the most overtly political poems in the collection are "The Little Black Boy" and "The Chimney Sweeper" in *Songs of Innocence*. "The Little Black Boy" is almost certainly inspired partly by the inhumanity of the slave trade, which Blake unequivocally condemned. It begins with familiar and problematic racial imagery in which "black" is the negative of "white": *My mother bore me in the southern wild, / And I am black, but O! my soul is white, / White as an angel is the English child: But I am black as if bereav'd of light.* But then something interesting—remarkable for a poem published in 1789—happens. At the beginning of the fourth stanza, Blake puts our earthly existence in theological context: *And we are put on earth a little space, / That we may learn to bear the beams of love.* For Blake, our earthly existence is an act of mercy that prepares us to encounter the light of God's presence. In and of itself, that is not significantly different from imagery used by many mystics and some dissenting preachers. But Blake turns the table when he describes how this truth is learned. First the little black boy's mother teaches him: *For when our souls have learn'd the heat to bear / The cloud will vanish we shall hear his voice, / Saying: come out from the grove my love & care, And round my golden tent like lambs rejoice. // Thus did my mother say and kissed me.* Then it is the little black boy who becomes the teacher: *And thus I say to little English boy. / When I from black and he from white cloud free, / And round the tent of God like lambs we joy: // I'll shade him from the heat till he can bear, / To lean in joy upon our father's knee. / And then I'll stand and stroke his silver hair, / And be like him and he will then love me.* Consistent with his image of contraries, Blake sees the human form as simultaneously that in which the divine is revealed and a "cloud" from which we must finally be released to love God and each other. "The Chimney Sweeper" takes up the exploitation of children in its first stanza: *When my mother died I was very young, / And my father sold me while yet my tongue, / Could scarcely cry weep weep weep weep. / So your chimneys I sweep & in soot I sleep.* This, remember, is a song of *Innocence.* It ends with the bitterly ironic image of Tom the chimney sweeper cheerfully going off to "do his duty" while he dreams of a sweet by and by in which an angel releases children from coffins so they can fly off to their father in heaven. The companion poem in *Experience* reiterates the irony: *And because I am happy, & dance, & sing, / They think they have done me no injury: / And are gone to praise God & his Priest & King / Who make up a heaven of our misery.*

These are songs children sing, and they are written by a poet more conscious than most of how much cruelty, pain, and violence can be wrapped up in the joyful noise of child's play. That the songs are also saturated with the music of Scripture (particularly the parallelism and repetition of the psalms as translated in the King James Version) and the music of English hymnody is an important key to understanding the critical eye Blake cast on his society. He had no doubt that one must become a child to see God, and he seems to have been convinced that children were more often attuned to his vision than adults. But he was careful to distinguish becoming children from the childishness of superficial promises that all would be happy if we simply did our "duty" as defined by the powers that be. The sequence of poems that begins with "The Little Boy Lost" and continues through "The Divine Image" recalls the story of Hagar and Ishmael being driven, forgotten, into the desert, after the birth of Isaac. In that story as in these poems, it is the weeping of a child that gets God's attention. And God's attention leads Blake to a beautiful hymn that reminds us what keeps us singing: *And all must love the human form, / In heathen, turk or jew. / Where Mercy, Love & Pity dwell, / There God is dwelling too.*

Blake turned to a poetics of word and image to engage the world with imagination. *Thou art a Man. God is no more; / Thine own Humanity learn to adore*, Blake wrote. And, in the voice of the daughters of Albion, *Arise, and drink your bliss, for every thing that lives is holy!* Strange words, perhaps, in a secular age marked by religious conflict that seems more inclined to drink destruction than bliss. But they may still move us to open our eyes to a world aflame and take off our shoes on holy ground.

Walking out of the Old Town School of Folk Music in Chicago after a performance by the Klezmatics of songs by Woody Guthrie, I overheard a young voice in the crowd scoffing at the idea of Holy Ground. "That," he said, "is the problem. There's too much of it." But I think he missed the point. When every war is pronounced holy, it is a sign that the ground is not. Harry S. Truman invoked God when he explained what had taken place in Hiroshima on 6 August 1945. Osama bin Laden invoked God to explain what took place in New York on 11 September 2001. If each grain of dust stirred up by those events, those that passed between, and those since is holy ground, it should most certainly give us pause. That it has not is a failure, and the first step in addressing it is to stop long enough to take off our shoes: "Don't just do something," said the Buddha. "Stand there."

As passing through ethics is the difference between immediate and immediate *again*, passing through Blake's *vision*, Coleridge's *active imagination*, is the difference between Woody Guthrie's 1954 pause for the holy and another pause introduced to the English speaking world in 1954, that of Vladimir and Estragon. The difference makes all the difference, and, for now, we have nothing more with which to begin.

Well? Shall we go?

X

¶The context in which Bergson speaks of the halo of intuition around intelligence suggests that he intends to connect intuition with instinct. This is consistent with the direction both he and James take in their descriptions of the noetic quality of mystical experience. Mystical experience is a knowing that cannot, simply, be said. And, though this means it must *be* experience, always directly experienced, it does not fit easily into a category of knowledge built up from sensory experience. It is more nearly equivalent to a ground on which (or a space within which) knowledge is constructed—and its validity consists in its resonance with a natural world governed not by freedom but by necessity. In another mystical tradition, this inexpressible is expressed in the idea that a Dao that could be otherwise would not be the Dao. It is a matter, as John Cage put it, of imitating Nature in her manner of operation. Bergson's *intuition*, though, like Laozi, makes a stronger statement still: not to imitate, but to *be* nature, because one cannot *not* be.

Nature is nothing if not creative, and Bergson locates its creativity in an evolutionary process that he depicts as an explosion of life in matter. He speaks of an *"original impetus* of life that passes from one generation to another through the developed organisms which bridge the interval between the generations. This impetus is sustained right along the lines of evolution among which it gets divided" and is "the fundamental cause of variations" that "accumulate and create new species." Species generally accentuate divergence as they evolve; but, if there is a common impetus, as Bergson claims, they must evolve identically in some points. To make this case, he turns to the evolution of the eye.

Taking note of two equally striking characteristics of the eye, "the complexity of its structure and the simplicity of its function," Bergson charts a course between simplicity and complexity, structure and form. The point is not to choose one or the other but to properly account for the rhythms by which they are related. In the case of the eye, it is a "contrast between the complexity of the organ and the unity of the function" that "gives us pause." Mechanistic theories would describe the evolution of the eye as a "gradual building-up of the machine under the influence of external influences intervening either directly by action on the tissues or indirectly by the selection of better-adapted ones." But even if such a theory is able to account for "the detail of the parts," it can do nothing to illuminate their correlation. Finalism would step in here to explain the coming together of the parts by "a preconceived plan with a view to a certain end."

Bergson maintains that both theoretical approaches

are anthropomorphic, attributing to Nature a mode of activity identical to the way in which a human actor would assemble a machine. Both the description of the organ as a machine and the identification of the evolution of the organ as an assembly of parts are problematic. With regard to the assembly of parts, Bergson notes that "a mere glance at the development of an embryo" will show that life does not work this way: "Life does not proceed by the association and addition of elements, but by dissociation and division."

Having dismissed mechanism and finalism as equally anthropomorphic, he returns to the "contrast between the infinite complexity of the organ and the extreme simplicity of the function" as the key to going beyond both. When an object appears as simple in one aspect, complex in another, the aspects do not generally have "the same degree of reality." The simplicity, he says, "belongs to the object itself," while the complexity belongs "to the views we take in turning around it, to the symbols by which our senses or intellect represent it to us, or, more generally, to elements *of a different order*, with which we try to imitate it artificially, but with which it remains incommensurable, being of a different nature."

To illustrate, Bergson imagines imitating the work of an artist who has painted a figure by means of mosaic tiles. The smaller the tiles, the better the imitation. But the tiles would have to be infinite and infinitely small to duplicate the original figure exactly. Now, if we were only capable of seeing the original as though it were composed of mosaic tiles, we might speak simply of a collection of mosaics, after the manner of the mechanistic hypothesis. We might also insist on a plan that guided the work of the artist, after the manner of finalism. But we would, in both cases, fail to see the real process of making the original picture.

Mechanism and finalism both divert attention from the process, movement, which Bergson insists is reality itself. Both go too far in one aspect, not far enough in another: "There is in vision more than the component cells of the eye and their mutual co-ordination: in this sense, neither mechanism nor finalism go far enough. But, in another sense, mechanism and finalism both go too far, for they attribute to Nature the most formidable of the labors of Hercules in holding that she has exalted to the simple act of vision an infinity of infinitely complex elements, whereas Nature has had no more trouble in making an eye than I have in lifting my hand. Nature's simple act has divided itself automatically into an infinity of elements which are then found to be co-ordinated to one idea, just as the movement of my hand has dropped an infinity of points which are then found to satisfy one equation." We have difficulty seeing this, Bergson suggests, because we conceive organization as manufacturing; but organization and manufacturing are not the same thing. Manufacturing is a human activity that consists of assembling parts in such a way as to produce a common action. The parts are arranged "around the action as an ideal center." To manufacture is to work "from the periphery to the center, or from the many to the one." Organization, on the other hand, works "from the center to the periphery."

The deeper difference between manufacturing and organization, though, is that the manufactured thing "delineates exactly the form of the work of manufacturing it... The whole of the result represents the whole of the work; and to each part of the work corresponds a part of the result." While approaching organization in these terms—treating the organized thing as though it were manufactured—is essential to science, which is not concerned with "the essence of things" but with "the best means of acting on them," this is a distortion of the work of organization. Bergson maintains that "the whole of an organized machine may, strictly speaking, represent the whole of the organizing work (this is, however, only approximately true), yet the parts of the machine do not correspond to parts of the work, because *the materiality of this machine does not represent a sum of means employed, but a sum of obstacles avoided.*" So, while "vision is a power which should attain by right an infinity of things inaccessible to our eyes," it is, in fact "canalized" for the sake of effectiveness. The visual apparatus "simply symbolizes the work of canalizing." Trying to explain the visual apparatus by the mere "assembling of its anatomic elements" is like trying to explain the digging of a canal "by the heaping-up of the earth which might have formed its banks." Mechanism would insist that the earth had been brought one cartload at a time, finalism that the cartloads had not been dumped at random. Both would be wrong.

Returning to the idea of the *organized machine* as a sum of obstacles avoided, Bergson modifies his comparison of nature's construction of the eye with our raising of a hand. Rather than assuming that the hand is raised with no resistance, he suggests that we imagine a hand being raised through a mass of iron filings "which are compressed and offer resistance to it in proportion as it goes forward." At the point where the hand has exhausted its effort, "the filings will be massed and coordinated in a certain definite form." If we suppose that the hand and the arm are not visible to onlookers, then they "will seek the reason of the arrangement in the filings themselves and in forces within the mass." Mechanists "will account for the position of each filing by the action exerted on it by the neighboring filings." Finalists will claim that "a plan of the whole has presided over the detail of these elementary actions.... But the truth is that there has been merely one indivisible act, that of the hand passing through the filings." Think of the arrangement of the filings as effect, the movement of the hand as cause, and it is true that "the whole of the effect is explained by the whole of the cause," but the parts of the effect do not correspond to the parts of the cause. The relation of vision to the eye, Bergson maintains, is analogous to the relation of the hand to the iron filings; and this means that "the form of the organ only expresses the degree in which the exercise of the function has been obtained."

Bergson is aware that speaking of "a progress toward vision" may open him to the charge of reintroducing finality. But this would only be the case if this progress required "the conscious or unconscious idea of an end to be attained." It doesn't. It depends rather on the "original impetus of life" and is "implied in this movement itself." It is implied in the movement, because "life is, more than anything else, a tendency to act on inert matter." Because the direction of action is not predetermined, the variety of forms generated is unforeseeable. But the action "presents, to some extent, the character of contingency; it implies at least a rudiment of choice. Now a choice involves the anticipatory idea of several possible actions. Possibilities of action must therefore be marked out for the living being before the action itself. Visual perception is nothing else: the visible outlines of bodies are the design of our eventual action on them. Vision will be found, therefore, in different degrees in the most diverse animals, and it will appear in the same complexity of structure wherever it has reached the same degree of intensity."

This recalls another illustration: "The finished portrait is explained by the features of the model, by the nature of the artist, by the colors spread out on the palette; but, even with the knowledge of what explains it, no one, not even the artist, could have foreseen exactly what the portrait would be, for to predict it would have been to produce it before it was produced—an absurd hypothesis which is its own refutation." Speaking here of individuals, Bergson writes that "It is then right to say that what we do depends on who we are; but it is necessary to add also that we are, to a certain extent, what we do, and that we are creating ourselves continually." This continuous self-creation is a microcosmic reflection of the macrocosmic process by which evolution proceeds, and it is equally true of all conscious beings: "...for a conscious being, to exist is to change, to change is to mature, to mature is to go on creating oneself endlessly."

In the end, the impetus of life, "consists in a need of creation. It cannot create absolutely, because it is confronted with matter, that is to say with the movement that is the inverse of its own. But it seizes upon this matter, which is necessity itself, and strives to introduce into it the largest possible amount of indetermination and liberty." *L'elan vital* explodes in matter, and the world, including us, becomes the body of creativity.

XI

¶Bergson envisions evolution as an explosive unfolding of life in matter, moving freely between the metaphor of a bomb and that of a musical composition where the explosion is a matter of creativity dancing around a pervasive theme. He turns to the image of an explosion at least in part to counter the linearity of evolutionary theory. Life, he says, is not a single course but a shell "which suddenly bursts into fragments, which fragments, being themselves shells, burst in their turn into fragments destined to burst again, and so on for a time incommensurably long. We perceive only what is nearest to us, the scattered movements of the pulverized explosions. From them we have to go back, stage by stage, to the original movement." It is not a matter of retracing a line, but rather of gathering fragments, tracing their paths back to a whole now fragmented, attending all the while to the patterns of their dispersion. In thinking about evolution, as in thinking about any other explosion, there are two series of causes to be considered: the resistance the explosion (in this case life) meets from inert matter and the explosive force itself. We are not dealing with the aftermath of a single explosion completed in some past time. If life is a bomb, it is a cluster bomb, and the explosions continue as long as life itself continues.

Our perception is local, so any account we base on perception will be constructed by extension from the center of our own experience. This demands a humility of explanation analogous to the humility Bergson attributes to life, which he says, has extended itself at least in part by making itself "very small and very insinuating, bending to physical and chemical forces, consenting even to go a part of the way with them, like the switch that adopts for a while the direction of the rail it is endeavoring to leave." At times, this makes it difficult to distinguish life from inert matter; but it also enables life to form that matter in ways that are both subversive and pervasive. The same could be said of the relation between Bergson's theory and mechanism. He goes some way with it, paying due respect to matter, but turning it on consciousness to make something more complex, more interesting, and more nearly true.

This theory steers between mechanism and finalism, both of which simplify and distort the process of life. As is fitting to evolutionary theory, Bergson begins observationally, turning his attention to two streams. "If we could speak," he says, "otherwise than metaphorically, of an impulse toward social life, it might be said that the brunt of the impulse was borne along the line of evolution ending at man, and that the rest of it was collected on the road leading to the *hymenoptera*: the societies of ants and bees would thus present the aspect complementary to ours." One cannot so speak, he says, but in a manner of speaking, though "there has been no particular impulse toward social life," tracing the new forms created by a single impulse on divergent lines can provide some insight into the process. And Bergson sees human society and insect societies as two such lines with particular promise.

Tracing the lines, Bergson steers clear of mechanism: "it is one thing," he writes, "to recognize that outer circumstances are forces evolution must reckon with, another to claim that they are the directing causes of evolution." Adaptation, in the sense of adjusting to the constraints of inert matter, "explains the sinuosities of the movement of evolution, but not its general direction, still less the movement itself." The particular twists and turns are so fascinating that they can divert our attention from the road as a whole; and they are so important to the shape of the road that it is tempting to think of them as its cause. But Bergson maintains that we must look elsewhere. In a variation on the theme of explosion, Bergson maintains that if "evolution is a creation unceasingly renewed, it creates, as it goes on, not only the forms of life, but the ideas that will enable the intellect to understand it, the terms which will serve to express it. That is to say that its future overflows its present, and cannot be sketched out therein as an idea."

Once again, this is a counsel of humility. Life, as a *tendency*, overflows every idea intended to contain it in every present, and so it is critical to recognize a sort of self-consuming corrective built into every idea of life. At the very least, this corrective should sweep mechanism off its feet; but it also undermines finalism. "Nature," Bergson writes, "is more and better than a plan in course of realization. A plan is a term assigned to a labor: it closes the future whose form it indicates. Before the evolution of life, on the contrary, the portals of the future remain wide open." Insistence on this openness is a mark of what Deleuze termed *Bergsonism*. Neither the beginning nor the end contains the explosive creativity of the process.

Within the single explosive evolutionary process, Bergson traces a number of divergent paths. He begins with the broad distinction between plant and animal, noting that there is no definite characteristic that distinguishes them. In the biological sciences, "the group must not be defined by the possession of certain characters, but by its tendency to emphasize them." So rather than looking for a single characteristic or group of characteristics by which to distinguish plant from animal, Bergson looks for distinguishable tendencies. Recall that he has already asserted that life is a tendency; now he suggests that it is a tendency properly composed of tendencies. This is one indication of the underlying unity of life: plant and animal diverge from a common source, and, because each retains traces of this origin, it cannot be entirely distinguished from others that share the traces as well as the origin.

So Bergson begins with a divergence of tendencies, equally legitimate strategies for securing solar energy, which is, ultimately, the single source of energy available for life on earth: the vegetable derives "elements necessary to maintain life" directly, while the animal assimilates these elements only after they have been fixed directly or indirectly by plants. This means that "ultimately the vegetable nourishes the animal." And it leads to a second set of divergent tendencies, mobility in the animal, fixity in the vegetable. This, in turn, leads to distinction in the degree of consciousness, because, as Bergson notes, there is an "obvious relationship" between mobility and consciousness. The animal has to move in order to secure nourishment, while the vegetable (generally speaking) does not. The ability to move in such a way as to secure nourishment requires a high degree of coordination—the kind afforded (generally speaking) by a more developed and centralized nervous system. And the more developed and centralized the nervous system, the more consciousness in the organism. Even "the humblest organism is conscious in proportion to its power to move *freely*." One thing leads to another, but not in a straight line. What begins as a unified life force in inert matter diverges on the basis of two strategies for securing nourishment from one environment. The two strategies lead to further divergence associated with degree of consciousness. It is possible to "define the animal by sensibility and awakened consciousness, the vegetable by consciousness asleep and by insensibility." Note that this is a distinction of tendency, not characteristic. All characteristics of life are inherent in both animal and vegetable; but the tendencies that define each make the characteristics more or less prominent. What is asleep in one is fully awake in the other.

The model that Bergson develops is holistic all the way down. Tendencies and capacities are not abandoned in the course of development but transformed, so that, in a sense, everything contains everything: we live in a universe of wholes in which division into parts is always a distortion. Divide these wholes, and every result remains a whole. Bergson expresses this in the form of a law: "When a tendency splits up in the course of its development, each of the special tendencies which thus arise tries to preserve and develop everything in the primitive tendency that is not incompatible with the work for which it is specialized." Evolution progresses as a rhythm of dissociation and incorporation (a controlled explosion, more like a burst of Liszt than the burst of a bomb).

Bergson identifies "two powers," instinct and intelligence, "immanent in life and originally intermingled, which were bound to part company in course of growth." And he identifies these powers particularly with social insects and human beings. "The evolution of the arthropods," he writes, "reaches its culminating point in the insect, and in particular in the *hymenoptera*, as that of vertebrates in man. Now, since instinct is nowhere so developed as in the insect world, and in no group of insects so marvelously as in the *hymenoptera*, it may be said that the whole evolution of the animal kingdom, apart from retrogressions toward vegetative life, has taken place on two divergent paths, one of which led to instinct and the other to intelligence." Three elements coincide in the vital impulse common to plants and animals: vegetative torpor, instinct, and intelligence. The "cardinal error which, from Aristotle onwards, has vitiated most of the philosophies of nature, is to see in vegetative, instinctive and rational life, three successive degrees of the development of one and the same tendency, whereas they are three divergent directions of an activity that has split up as it grew. The difference between them is not a difference of intensity, nor, more generally, of degree, but of kind." Vegetable and animal life are "at once mutually complementary and mutually antagonistic," as are intelligence and instinct. Neither is ever found in its pure state, and so our attention is directed to tendencies, not things. Philosophically, this inclines Bergson "to replace the rigidity of a diagram by the suppleness of life." Edges bend, blur; categories shift.

In Bergson's model, the world is permeated by "vegetative torpor," instinct, and intelligence. One does not succeed or exclude the other; all are present in every manifestation of life. There is no doubt that "there is intelligence wherever there is inference; but inference, which consists in an inflection of past experience in the direction of present experience, is already a beginning of invention. Invention becomes complete when it is materialized in a manufactured instrument." Tools, then, and their use, become one of the ways in which Bergson distinguishes between instinct and intelligence. "Intelligence," he writes, "considered in what seems to be its original feature, is the faculty of manufacturing artificial objects, especially tools to make tools, and of indefinitely varying the manufacture." One of the most important distinctions between particular lives in which intelligence is ascendant and those dominated by instinct is that intelligence is directed toward creating tools with which to use the natural world, while instinct is directed toward using the body and its organs. Bergson puts it this way: "instinct perfected is a faculty of using and even constructing organized instruments; intelligence perfected is the faculty of making and using unorganized instruments." The tool is, effectively, an "artificial organ," and the distinction is between tending to use organs that are artificial and tending to use organs that are "natural" to appropriate or consume the world.

None of this should be read as construing mutually exclusive categories or establishing a rigidly hierarchical relationship. Bergson notes that "intelligence has even more need of instinct than instinct has of intelligence; for the power to give shape to crude matter involves already a superior degree of organization, a degree to which the animal could not have risen, save on the wings of instinct." The point is that instinct and intelligence "represent two different solutions, equally fitting, of one and the same problem." Furthermore, "instinct and intelligence imply two radically different kinds of knowledge."

Though it might appear that instinct is more closely related to the unconscious, intelligence to consciousness, Bergson rejects this conclusion, arguing instead that both instinct and intelligence are related to consciousness, which in turn has to be related to the unconscious. He distinguishes two kinds of unconsciousness, "that in which consciousness is *absent*, and that in which consciousness is *nullified*." On the flip side of this, Bergson says that "the consciousness of a living being may be defined as an arithmetical difference between potential and real activity. It measures the interval between representation and action."

Note that the key relationship here is between action (associated with instinct) and representation (associated with intelligence). What matters most is the interval between the two, meaning, in terms familiar from Jean Piaget's epistemological investigations, that with expanding consciousness comes an expanding ability to separate representation from action. In instinctual knowledge, the two collapse almost entirely into one another; intelligence tends to pull them apart: "while instinct and intelligence both involve knowledge, this knowledge is rather *acted* and unconscious in the case of instinct, *thought* and conscious in the case of intelligence. The essential difference is a matter of orientation to the object. In instinct, knowledge is implicit; in intelligence, there is no innate knowledge of any object, but there is knowledge of relations. So whatever passes as innate knowledge in instinct bears on things while in intelligence it bears on relations." Put another way, "intelligence, in so far as it is innate, is the knowledge of a form; instinct implies the knowledge of a matter." Instinctive knowledge is formulated in categorical propositions, while intellectual knowledge is expressed hypothetically.

In keeping with the generally transcendent impetus of life, "an intelligent being bears within itself the means to transcend" her or his own nature. This is not accomplished by discarding instinct. There are things "that intelligence alone is able to seek, but which, by itself, it will never find. These things instinct alone could find; but it will never seek them." So there must be an interplay of the two. Intellect aims first at constructing. As it leaves the hand of nature, Bergson says, our intelligence "has for its chief object the unorganized solid. It forms clear ideas only of the discontinuous." In fact, the intellect systematically (but understandably) distorts nature by starting from immobility and forming its idea of movement by constructing it out of "immobilities put together." It is only of immobility that the intellect can "form a clear idea." The intellect is always stepping back, isolating states and recombining them in order to comprehend. Instinct moves in, remains always local, so that the instinctive sign is *adherent*. Intellect, stepping back, attends to relations, delocalizes, and constructs signs that are *mobile*. Both instinct and intelligence treat matter as an instrument of action, an organ. Intellect, always in the process of separating in space, fixes in time.

Despite its best efforts, "the intellect is characterized by a natural inability to comprehend life." Life always overflows conceptual containment; but comprehension is more nearly accessible to instinct, which is organic, than to intelligence, which is mechanical. Intelligence typically tries to understand the world as a machine, by turning it into a machine. But the world is an organism and must be comprehended as such, if it is comprehended at all.

It is not surprising, then, that Bergson turns to a faculty, intuition, associated with instinct rather than intelligence as critical for encountering the pure movement of the world. Continuing to map the relationship between instinct and intelligence as forms of knowledge, he notes that "life, as soon as it has become bound up in a species, is cut off from the rest of its own work, save at one or two points that are of vital concern to the species just arisen. Is it not plain that life goes to work here exactly like consciousness, exactly like memory? We trail behind us, unawares, the whole of our past; but our memory pours into the present only the odd recollection or two that in some way complete our present situation. Thus the instinctive knowledge which one species possesses of another on a certain particular point has its root in the very unity of life, which is, to use the expression of an ancient philosopher, a 'whole sympathetic to itself.'"

The cell relates to other cells, species relate to other species, as consciousness relates to the past—only attending to those small portions of it that are immediately relevant to action in the present. But that instinctive knowledge, with its root in the unity of life, resists reabsorption into intelligence when intelligence sets out to reconstruct the whole from parts it has isolated. Intelligence proceeds step by step, in the way that one might establish distance via touch. But instinct proceeds in a flash, after the manner of vision. Instinct "has the same relation to intelligence that vision has to touch." And, as he so often does, Bergson connects this with the flow of music—theme and variations, apprehended as a whole, hearing the first note only when we have heard the last. And, though they are undeniably related, the way we hear music differs radically from the way we see it.

Intelligence is a faculty perfectly suited to "relating one point of space to another, one material object to another;

it applies to all things, but remains outside them; and of a deep cause it perceives only the effects spread out side by side." Instinct, on the other hand, is sympathy, best suited to approaching wholes. And thus it is that instinct leads to intuition, "instinct that has become disinterested, self-conscious, capable of reflecting upon its object and of enlarging it indefinitely." Intelligence is an eye to read music, instinct an ear to hear it. Cultivated, intelligence is a critical faculty, instinct an aesthetic one. Both together are necessary to fully encounter the explosion of "consciousness launched into matter: if intelligence is charged with matter and instinct with life, we must squeeze them both in order to get the double essence from them..."

XII

¶ As a model of how to extend perception, Bergson pointed to art, which he saw as enabling a deeper and broader perception by displacing attention—a function he also saw as appropriate to philosophy. Attention is one of the ways in which "the necessities of action tend to limit the field of vision." The artist, absent-mindedly less attached to and preoccupied with "the positive and material side of life" is more open to a broader range of experience. Bergson describes our "normal psychological life as a constant effort of the mind to limit its horizon, to turn away from what it has a material interest in not seeing." In terms of time and change, this means turning away from the flow in which we are constantly immersed to "distinct perceptions" that are "cut, for the purposes of practical existence, out of a wider canvas." Philosophy, he argues, like art, can "lead us to a completer perception of reality by means of a certain displacement of our attention... *turning* this attention *aside* from the part of the universe which interests us from a practical viewpoint and *turning it back* toward what serves no practical purpose."

He notes that this sounds very much like what philosophy has purported to do since Plato, but he has something different in mind. He takes Plotinus, who said that "all action weakens contemplation," as exemplary of the Platonic spirit. In that spirit, Plotinus "demanded a conversion of the mind, which breaks away from the appearances here below and attaches itself to the realities above." The point, Bergson says, was to transport oneself "into a world different from the one we inhabit," to cultivate "faculties of vision other than those we constantly exercise in the knowledge of the external world and of ourselves." Because Kant "disputed the existence of these transcendent faculties, he believed metaphysics to be impossible." If it were possible, he maintained, it would be "through a vision and not through a dialectic." It would require "a superior intuition, a perception," Bergson says, of "metaphysical reality." And in this, he maintains, Kant was right, though he was mistaken to turn that, surprisingly, in the Platonic direction of desire to rise above change. Bergson argues that Kant made the same mistake as his metaphysical adversaries because they "imagined that our senses and consciousness, as they function in everyday life, make us grasp movement directly." Beginning with this assumption, they took the fact that "in following the usual data of our senses and consciousness we arrive in the speculative order at insoluble contradictions" as an indication that "contradiction was inherent in change itself" and that to avoid such contradiction "one had to get out of the sphere of change and lift oneself above Time." But Bergson maintains that the metaphysicians and their Kantian opponents share a fundamental misperception of change.

He locates the source of the misperception in Eleatic philosophy and especially in the paradoxes by which Zeno of Elea demonstrated the absurdity of movement. But Zeno's *movement* was neither movement nor change. It was a crystallization of the perception of movement, "a solidification with an eye to practice." And Kant's *time* was "a time which neither flows nor changes nor endures." The problem is not how to get outside of time (which is precisely what our ordinary perception is designed to do). The problem is how to get inside it. This means, for Bergson, that we must "grasp change and duration in their original mobility."

This turn is critical. By making "a strenuous effort to put aside some of the artificial schema we interpose unknowingly between reality and us," by breaking "certain habits of thinking and perceiving that have become natural to us," Bergson believes we can "return to the direct perception of change and mobility." One result of this return is that we will "think of all change, all movement, as being absolutely indivisible." That we can return to the kind of direct perception of change Bergson envisions and that this will lead us to think of change as absolutely indivisible are equally critical. "Movement," he writes, "is reality itself"; and much of our confusion about it derives from the same confusion Bergson attributes to Zeno, a confusion of movement with the space that it covers.

He imagines Achilles's commentary on overtaking the tortoise. Zeno's mistake, Achilles says, is "making movement and immobility coincide." This is the habit of thinking that we must overcome: "We argue about movement as though it were made of immobilities and, when we look at it, it is with immobilities that we reconstitute it." Bergson attributes this to an "instinctive fear of those difficulties which the vision of movement as movement would arouse in our thought." If movement is, as Bergson maintains, reality itself, then ordinary existence requires that we treat indivisible change "as a series of distinct states which form, as it were, a line in time... If change is continuous in us and also in things..., in order that the uninterrupted change which each of us calls 'me' may act upon the uninterrupted change that we call a 'thing,'" these two changes have to be like two trains whose motions are so coordinated that they are stationary relative to one another. When "the two changes, that of the object and that of the subject, take place under particular conditions, they produce the particular appearance that we call a 'state.' And once in possession of 'states,' our mind recomposes change with them." Breaking change into states makes it possible for us to act on things, but, Bergson writes, "what is favorable to action in this case would be fatal to speculation." There is nothing "below" movement, but the practical utility of states can fool us into treating them as though they were more fundamental, as though they were the constituent parts of which movement is made.

Part of our difficulty lies in the privileged position we accord vision, which is entirely dependent on discrete states. So Bergson turns to hearing, where melody gives us an experience more nearly analogous to pure motion—motion without a mobile, as it were. In a melody, the change is the thing itself, in spite of our inclination to divide it and picture it as "a juxtaposition of distinct notes." If the melody stops, it is "no longer the same sonorous whole" but "another, equally indivisible." With melody, as with movement or change, we always encounter wholes, never parts. One is reminded of Adorno's comment that we do not hear the first note of a Beethoven symphony until we hear the last. Since "real duration is what we have always called time," we encounter time whole. This poses practical problems for measurement as well as action and tempts us to the fixity of states. But Bergson maintains that change is more solid and substantial than fixity. The present instant, fixed, is a pure abstraction, "an ephemeral arrangement between mobilities"; as such, it is subject to immediate dissolution when attention shifts, as it invariably does.

The seemingly paradoxical solidity of change requires a different way of thinking about the past than the one to which we have grown accustomed. We have been inclined to think of the past as inexistent, and philosophers have encouraged this natural tendency. We think of the present alone existing (as, for example, in Augustine's familiar discussion of time in Book XI of his *Confessions*, where there is a present of things past, a present of things present, and a present of things to come), of the past surviving only in fragments, only "because of some act of charity on the part of the present—by the intervention of a certain particular function called memory." Now memory is understood as an act of the present, a preservation of parts of the past tucked away "in a kind of box." But this is a mistake. The present instant is to time what a point is to a line, a pure abstraction, an act of the mind with no real existence. But we think of the present not as an instant or as a point but as a duration, the limits of which are elusive. Bergson connects them with attention and maintains that "the distinction we make between our present and past is... at least relative to the extent of the field which our attention to life can embrace." The moment attention flags, the portion of the present "held under its gaze" becomes part of the past. The past, we might say, is present unless it is held momentarily at bay by a particular attention. Memory, therefore, does not require an explanation: "there is no special faculty whose role is to retain quantities of past in order to pour it into the present. The past preserves itself automatically." It is not remembering that requires a special account, but forgetting.

For Bergson, the continuity of change, the indivisibility of movement, translates into a continuity and indivisibility of inner life that means, in turn, that it is the "apparent abolition" of the past, not its preservation, that must be accounted for. And the account emerges from the structure of the brain itself. The function of the brain consists in "canalizing our attention in the direction of the future, in order to turn it away from the past—...that part of our history which does not concern our present actions—in order to bring to it at most, in the form of 'memories,' one simplification or another of anterior experience, destined to complete the experience of the moment." Bergson maintains (speaking not so much of structure as of function) that the brain chooses from the past, diminishes it, simplifies it, utilizes it, but does not preserve it. This, he says, would not be so difficult to believe "if we had not acquired the habit of believing that the past is abolished." On the contrary, the past can—and does—preserve itself automatically—and "preservation of the past in the present is nothing else than the indivisibility of change." In short, "reality is change, ...change is indivisible, and ...in an indivisible change the past is one with the present."

More than twenty years earlier, in *Time and Free Will*, Bergson arrived at time by way of number, which he understood as "a collection of units or the synthesis of the one and the many, but also as the simple intuition of a multiplicity of parts or units, which are absolutely alike." To picture number, "we are compelled to have recourse to an extended image"; it is the picturing that moves us from habits of counting in time toward the fixing of sums in space. He notes that "every clear idea of number implies a visual image in space; and the direct study of the units which go to form a discrete multiplicity will lead us to the same conclusion on this point as the examination of number itself." Examining this in detail would distract us from time, the matter at hand; but it is worth noting the extent to which the action of mind on matter enters into Bergson's understanding of space, time, and the relationship between the two. He goes so far as to assert that an act of mind is required for the existence of space. There is an *intuition* of "an empty homogeneous medium"—and this intuition is extended to time, which is conceptualized as "an unbounded medium, different from space but homogeneous like the latter: the homogeneous is thus supposed to take two forms, according as its contents coexist or follow one another". Time is connected with succession, but there is a tendency to fall back on space, to give up on time by abstracting it from duration. Projected into space, time "is nothing but the ghost of space haunting the reflective consciousness." But there are two conceptions of time, one free from alloy, and one that surreptitiously brings in the idea of space.

It is the confusion of the two that poses a problem. Alluding to melody, Bergson insists that it is possible to conceive pure duration, though we tend to project time into space and abandon pure duration by attributing homogeneity to it. The moment one attributes "the least homogeneity to duration," one "surreptitiously introduces space." Bergson is quite willing to acknowledge a kind of time, *homogeneous time*, that, projected into space, becomes, effectively, its fourth dimension. But this is not the "real" time of pure duration. Science, by limiting time to homogeneous time, "eliminates duration from time, mobility from motion." But space alone is homogeneous: "objects in space form a discrete multiplicity," and "every discrete multiplicity is got up by a process of unfolding in space." But this discrete multiplicity is not the only variety and, in fact, "we cannot even form the idea of discrete multiplicity without considering at the same time a qualitative multiplicity." Qualitative multiplicity is a characteristic of mind, and its subsumption under the quantitative is a materialization of time. It is via motion that "duration assumes the form of a homogeneous medium, and that time is projected into space." Duration is perceived as quality not quantity by immediate consciousness "and it retains this form so long as it does not give place to a symbolical representation derived from extensity."

The act of symbolization involves extension, spatialization; it tends toward the numerical multiplicity of homogeneous duration. But before the symbol, there is qualitative multiplicity, "a duration whose heterogeneous moments permeate one another." Parallel to this, there is at one and the same time, a self with well defined states and a self in which "succeeding each other means melting into one another and forming an organic whole." Again, it is the confusion that is problematic: "consciousness, goaded by an insatiable desire to separate, substitutes the symbol for the reality, or perceives the reality only through the symbol." The result is not only spatialized or materialized time, which is effectively a fourth dimension of space, but also the suppression of "real" time, the disappearance of duration, replaced by the space in which motion takes place.

When Bergson returned to these issues in 1922, in *Duration and Simultaneity*, Einstein was on his mind; but he had not abandoned the line of thought initiated decades earlier. Time, he wrote, is at first "identical with the continuity of our inner life: a self-sufficient flow or passage, the flow not implying a thing that flows, and the passing not presupposing states through which we pass; the thing and the state are only artificially taken snapshots of the transition; and the transition, all that is naturally experienced, is duration itself." Perception appears to be inside and out at the same time, and the question is how to pass the inner time of pure duration to the time of things.

Bergson answers with reference to our status as embodied beings. Moments of inner life correspond to moments of the body. We work out from the personal consciousness of pure duration toward "an impersonal consciousness that is the link among all individual consciousnesses." He accepts "the hypothesis of a physical time that is one and universal," convinced that Einstein's theory "was, if anything, meant to bear out the idea of a time common to all things." But he does not stop at simply physical time—which, as has already been suggested, is more properly a kind of space. "What we wish to establish," he writes, "is that we cannot speak of a reality that endures without inserting consciousness into it."

This is by way of memory, which is indistinguishable from duration, "a continuation of what no longer exists into what does exist." It is the continuation, the unfolding, that is primary; and without the unfolding there would be nothing but space. When we measure "time," we measure the space into which our consciousness projects it. Every duration, Bergson says, "is thick; real time has no instants." Like a point where a line is brought to an end, "the instant is what would terminate duration if the latter came to a halt. But it does not halt. Real time cannot therefore supply the instant; the latter is borne of the mathematical point, that is to say, of space." The instant, instantaneity, "involves two things, a continuity of real time, that is duration, and a Spatialized time, that is, a line which, described by a motion, has thereby become symbolic of time."

Bergson repeats two propositions fundamental to his

argument: first, it is "the simultaneity between two instants of two motions outside us that allows us to measure
an interval of time"; and, second, "it is the simultaneity of
these moments with moments dotted by them along our
inner duration that makes this measurement one time."
Measuring time consists in "counting simultaneities." Science "counts instants, takes note of simultaneities, but
remains without a grip on what happens in the intervals."

We empty time into a space of four dimensions because
the only way we are able to "measure" time is by replacing it with simultaneities "which we count." But if our science thereby limits itself to space. "it is easy to see why the
dimension of space that has come to replace time is still
called time. It is because our consciousness is there." And
the stuff of our consciousness is time, which, if we keep, as
Bergson advises, to experience, we can experience without simply collapsing it into symbolic-conventional time
that is no more than a fourth dimension of space.

XIII

¶ That instants are abstracted from real duration partly
explains the ineffability of mystical experience. To *say* is
to abstract a moment from process, to *place* it (though this
might misleadingly be referred to as freezing the moment
in time). It is to tempt the hearer to see the static abstraction in place of the moving experience. Piaget's description of the equilibration of cognitive structure as punctuated equilibrium, like James's description of perchings
in flights of consciousness, partly addresses this. Because
the perch appears more solid than flight, it is tempting to
think perching more real than flying. But consciousness
construed as no more than an assembly of perchings never
takes flight.

For the mystic who ventures to speak of experience beyond words, this invites the kind of acerbic criticism Bertrand Russell leveled at Wittgenstein, who, he noted, was able to say a great deal about what he said could not be said. *About* is the key word. Wittgenstein had no need to worry about writing about what he said could not be said because what cannot be said *must* be unspoken. One must read *about* it, between the lines. Laozi could write roughly five thousand characters after *dao ke dao feichang dao* because he had no reason to confuse them with *dao*: writing about a way is not the way, but the way one writes is a *gesture*. And the gesture is characteristic of the knowing of mysticism, which is more akin to the knowing of a paper wasp than what is typically named "knowing" in human beings. The wasp knows in her doing, which is all we see: there is no interval of space between the knowing and the doing. A human observer may describe what the wasp does; but she, together with the whole colony, makes a nest and lives in it.

I have nothing to say, John Cage wrote,   *and I am saying it*   *and that is poetry*   *as I need it.* In his "Lecture on Nothing," Cage speaks of recording that gets in the way of music:

A lady   *from Texas*   *said:*   *I live in Texas*   .
    We have no music   *in Texas.*
    The reason they've no
music in Texas   *is because*   *they have recordings*
in Texas.   *Remove the records from Texas*
    and someone   *will learn to sing*   .
    Everybody   *has a song*
    which is   *no*   *song at all*   :
    it is a process   *of singing*   ,
    and when you sing   ,
    you are   *where you are*   .

> *All I know about method is that when I am not working I sometimes think I know something, but when I am working, it is quite clear that I know nothing.*

Exactly. A gesture invites. What we call knowing most often stops to describe, and that, as Bergson knows, is critical. It says what we think we know. But to know as a mystic like Julian knows is to fly. And that is poetry, as we need it.

FOUR
The Power of the Powerless

¶One close reading after another of Václav Havel's "Power of the Powerless" has led me to the conclusion that the best—and closest—way to read Havel is to cast a critical eye on what goes without saying in the worlds we inhabit, to make scenes in it, as playwrights do (even when they go, as Havel did, to the castle) wherever and whenever we can. So what follows will weave together readings of the world that you might recognize as "lecture" with lyric poetry that you might not. I hope you find what you don't recognize unsettling enough to shed new light on what you do, unfinished as it is, so together we may find that, in fact, we don't.

I begin with a little something for Saint Francis, who will be in the background today, on the day after his feast day. It was written, by the way, on a day dedicated to another friar, Saint Bonaventure, who is always a good guide for close reading.

Sick and tired of being
sick and tired, I told
my wife I was looking in
to joining the Franciscans.
Knowing I am temperamentally
Trappist or anything discalced,
she said *what do they make you do*
and I said *nothing* then thought again
and said *preach good news to birds*
and she said *you do that already*
and (discounting the possibility
that she meant nothing) I said
nah, they preach to me.
I just say amen and
all this came to mind today
when a friend reminded

me this is Saint Bonaventure's
day and in his honor she is
trying to ignore little annoyances
but I suppose those would be
the ones a Franciscan scholar would embrace
(*suffer the little*, you know) and that got me thinking
about the mind's journey, the mind's journey in,
as I recall, not up, to God, present wherever
it was, said a preacher of another order
but a like mind, you left the divine,
which could be anywhere.

Turn, turn. Take off your shoes.
Every step you step you step on holy ground.

I just returned from driving almost three thousand miles
across Illinois, Missouri, Oklahoma, Texas, and Kansas for
a series of readings and an art exhibit in Dodge City. This
loop through the middle of America had me thinking—as
it almost always does—of the traditional story of how the
daodejing—the book of the power of the way—came to be.
As the story is told, laozi, who was a member of the Chinese court, became disillusioned with politics and headed
west until he came to a border crossing, where the guard
recognized him and demanded that he write down what
he knew before he would be allowed to cross to the other
side. (If you imagine a map of China marked by a journey
west from the center of power, you can also imagine the
other side to which laozi was crossing was Lhasa—Tibet,
which creates an interesting field in which to contemplate
power.) What laozi wrote down in this traditional tale is
the *daodejing* we know, eighty-one little gems, lyric poems
that continue to be read and translated and pondered by

people around the world today. The moral of the story, you might say, is to always carry a perfect square of poems in your pocket, because you never know when you will need them to get over a border.

It also brought to mind Harris Stone's *Dispersed City of the Plains*, in which the built objects of the human world on the high plains—attempts to solve problems—reveal a series of questions posed to human presencing by the natural environment. He approaches built forms "in such a way that an observer can draw a set of basic images from the cultural landscape. A derelict windmill, its fan rusted and immobile; a grain bin, its adjacent set of railroad tracks overgrown with weeds; an abandoned anti-ballistic missile site enclosed within a chain link fence capped with strands of barbed wire... if each of these images is viewed as a reaction to a problem, as an attempted solution, the outline of a series of questions begins to emerge. This questioning gaze at particular situations can penetrate the surface of things, their stylistic labels, and focus on the common experiences, the building practices and trends that give shape to built forms and are, in turn, modified by them." Material objects with which human beings mark an environment like the Great Plains are evidence of a conversation, and the conversation is a *polis*, even if the population density is (as it is in the county where I grew up) 1.5 persons per square mile. Part of what it means to be human in the world is to make cities and dwell in them—not necessarily by planning and choosing to do so but simply by addressing the world as a problem posed, as one problem after another. "What is striking and interesting about these built forms," Stone writes, "are the social relations which people have established among themselves in the course of transforming the landscape and the consequent transformation of the symbolic capability of their activity."

One of the elements Stone mentions as constitutive of the dispersed city of the plains is the windmill, a built object that has been transformed in the years since he died. When Stone identified the grain elevator, the barbed wire fence, and the windmill as primary built forms, the windmill he had in mind was the lone derelict, rusting and immobile. The windmills one encounters now are concentrated in centralized arrays designed to do what all those oil pumps scattered across Oklahoma and Texas have done—and often for the same people. The windmills that Stone pictured in his beautiful book are decentralized, focused on addressing the problem of dry in a particular place at a particular time. The massive windmills that now go on for miles and miles on the plains, tall as the Wrigley Building, are focused on moving power from here to there. That is a turn that marks not only the forces of dispersal that so intrigued Stone but also the forces of centralization characteristic of modern States. Gazing at windmills in Kansas makes me painfully aware of how appropriate it is that a book popular in the United States a number of years ago under the title *What's The Matter With Kansas?* was sold in the rest of the world under the title *What's the Matter With America?*

An army of crosses
four hundred feet tall rises
on a long mesa

beyond the Double Mountain Fork of the Brazos
river, triune blades turning in wind—could be a mass

crucifixion, a sign
to snuff out a revolution—
power droning one truth on and on

(amongst black billboards
with messages in white letters
signed GOD): *to die for the sins of the world is nothing*

unusual. What church do you believe
the world will make of it this time?

I

¶We enter the postapocalyptic world Russell Hoban
dreamed for Riddley Walker at a time when the hands on
the doomsday clock were closer to midnight according to
those who have used them to mark time since the begin‐
ning of the nuclear age—we enter in the middle of Rid‐
dley Walker's memory of the end of a hunt for a wild boar
when he turned twelve. We learn on the second line that
this wild boar is the last known to be living in the small
place Riddley inhabits. This is a rite of passage, and in it,
in the middle, the first thing we see is a memory of the end:

> "He done the reqwyrt he ternt and stood and clattert
> his teef and made his rush and there we wer then.
> Him on 1 end of the spear kicking his life out and me
> on the other end watching him dy. I said, 'Your tern
> now my tern later.' The other spears gone in then
> and he wer dead and the steam coming up off him in
> the rain and we all yelt, 'Offert!'
> The woal thing fealt jus that littl bit stupid. Us run‐
> ning that boar thru that las little scrump of woodling
> with the forms all roun. Cows mooing sheap baaing
> cocks crowing and us foraging our las boar in a thin
> grey girzel on the day I come a man."

Russell Hoban also dreamed Frances, a little badger who lives in some of my favorite books for children, perpetually entangled in the travails of everyday (presumably preapocalyptic) life. In *A Bargain for Frances*, she is tricked by a friend into buying a cheap plastic tea set when what she has been saving for is a tea set made of real china. Francis has a little song for everything (a bit like a Bollywood film), and walking home with her brand new plastic tea set before she knows she's been tricked, she sings *A plastic pot can pour the tea / For my dolls and friends and me / Just as well as china. / Red is just as good as blue. / Plastic cups are all right too, / Just as good as china.*

When she gets home, her little sister Gloria tells her the tea set is ugly and (with the matter of fact brutality many little sisters master in give and take with older siblings), she exposes the trick.

So Frances does what one does (especially if one has been a careful reader of Plato) when a dirty trick is brought to light. She sings a new song: *Now that plastic's what I've got, / Backsies are what there is not. / Mother told me to be careful, But Thelma better be bewareful.* Then she hatches a careful plan to set her friend up and get the tea set she really wants.

Which she does. A mean trick in response to a mean trick and Frances has what she's been saving for. Thelma (who should know a mean trick when she sees one) says "That is not a very nice trick to play on a friend." Frances, ever honest, does not deny it. And Thelma comes to the obvious conclusion, confirming what Mother said in the first place: "Well... from now on I will have to be careful when I play with you."

Putting aside for a moment the fact that a dirty trick has led to a dirty trick that put our hero back on track, this is the ending of countless children's books intended to be morally uplifting: always listen to your mother and always be careful out there.

Mother seems to be a wise and kind badger who has some experience of the ins and outs of play, so listening to her is not a bad idea. And, to her credit, Frances usually does. But that is not the end of it. "Being careful," Frances says, "is not as much fun as being friends. Do you want to be careful or do you want to be friends?"

The answer goes without saying. And, in good Aristotelian fashion, it ends in action that is a sign of practical wisdom. Having chosen to be friends, Thelma and Frances go back to Frances's house to skip rope. Little sister Gloria joins them. And Frances says "You and Gloria can skip first... I will go last."

The last scene of this Bollywood film is the whole cast dancing and singing *Careful once, careful twice, / Being careful is not nice. / Being friends is better.*

In the harsher world Riddley Walker inhabits, Russell Hoban has him put this another way—and this, for those of you who have been wondering, is why I begin here:

> "I cud feal some thing growing in me it wer like a grean sea surging in me it wer saying, LOSE IT. Saying, LET GO. Saying, THE ONLYES POWER IS NO POWER.
>
> There come in to my mynd then music or the idear of music I dont know what it wer if I try to hear it now I cant only I know I heard it then. It wer as much colours as it wer souns only if I try to see the colours now I cant. The souns and the colours they be come a moving and I thot I cud move with it."

That is not the last word—or, if it is, it comes again later, still in the middle of memory:

"Membering when that thot come to me: THE ON-LYES POWER IS NO POWER. Wel now I sust that werent qwite it. It aint that its no Power. Its the not sturgling for Power thats where the Power is. Its in jus letting your self be where it is..."

In darkness nearing midnight it is not difficult to conjure visions of cutting deals—and knowing the devil is in the details and even atomic clocks can be a bit off, it is not difficult to imagine deals done, especially where being where power is is concerned.

> Sky so big it needs the whole earth
> to lie down on. Paper said chance of rain
> today and tomorrow and tomorrow and tomorrow
> but thin high clouds say not likely, not
> today. River is out of sight,
> but it has broken flat
> into high mesas and deep arroyos
> trailing down down to where you
> would think water would be. A field of maize is
> green in the middle of ocher that shades
> from white through the color of alfalfa flowers
> to brown as brown as earth and gold
> as gold as wheat at harvest time.
> Mennonite Church on the edge of Perryton
> reminds me the opposite of a war story
> is an epic about farming.
>
> Conversation where I stop is Texas
> Tech football, sounds like something
> a zen master might say: *Tech is better than*
> *people think. They haven't played*

nobody but they've beat three nobodies
convincingly. A word or two about
growing up here, then the conversation turns
to banks. Guy at the table says
he's thinking about buying another one.

Owner of the coffee shop in Dodge City
offers me a fly swatter, talks about the oil boom
when I ask where all the traffic on
Wyatt Earp Boulevard is headed. I say
hope that works out. The problem with booms
is bust and he goes off on football players
salaries, says *it's all about managing money,*
and I wonder what would be the epic opposite that.

II

¶I am reluctant to call anything a permanent attribute of
anything, but it is perhaps correct to say that being haunted is a permanent aspect of human existence. (Since human existence is not permanent, a "permanent" aspect of it
ceases to be when human existence ceases to be.) Flannery
O'Connor spoke of the southern United States in terms
of this aspect, saying that, though it may not be Christ-
centered, it is certainly Christ-haunted. She demonstrated in her novels, particularly *Wise Blood.* William Goyen,
writing in East Texas, on the western edge of the south,
painted an equally brilliant, though less familiar, portrait
in *Come, the Restorer.* Václav Havel, with his unflinching
sense of the absurd, alludes to a world-historical claim of
haunting at the beginning of "The Power of the Powerless." The spectre he has in mind is not Communism but
"what in the West is called 'dissent'", and the arena of its
haunting is *Eastern* Europe, not the single Europe of the

Communist Manifesto. What I find most significant in each of these instances is the intuition that one way to get one's bearings in a place and time is to identify what haunts it—or, more properly, to tell a story in which the ghosts are visibly, tangibly present. Toni Morrison's *Beloved* is an exemplary ghost story in this sense, as are Mary Shelley's *Frankenstein* and Havel's *Temptation.*

But in the essay, the spectre haunting Eastern Europe is "what in the West is called dissent." (I repeat *what in the West is called* each time, not only for emphasis but also because it implies that, from where Havel writes, though this is what it is called *there* it may not be what it is *here.)* That particular ghost is the vehicle Havel rides to one of the most insightful works of political philosophy written in the twentieth century. It is often read simply as a critique of post 1968 Czechoslovakia. But it is more.

What haunts Havel's plays is the soul-numbing bureaucracy characteristic of post-totalitarianism. In "The Power of the Powerless," we encounter this first in the greengrocer who hangs a sign in his window that bears the slogan *Workers of the World Unite,* a common variant of the conclusion Marx and Engels come to in *The Communist Manifesto.* Havel begins with the greengrocer's act, which he undertakes not out of some heartfelt conviction about the world's workers but because the Party has mandated the sign. The presence of the sign allows him to go about his business. The absence of the sign would disturb the peace in which he does so. If you asked him why he hung the sign, the greengrocer would probably say this is simply the way things are done here and he sees no reason to make trouble. Havel's focus on doing things the way things are done here as a way to keep the peace and avoid trouble that would disrupt action is critical to his argument. It brings Aristotle to mind again, particularly his discussion of habit in the *Nicomachean Ethics*. Plato listens for the song when he wants to know the shape of the city. Aristotle looks for the habit. I like to believe we recognize the communities to which strangers belong by the habits that they wear and where they wear them.

The spectre that haunts eastern Europe is "a natural and inevitable consequence of the present historical phase of the system it is haunting." In that assertion, Havel adopts one of the most important habits of Marxist analysis—the habit of identifying ghosts in a machine as products of the working of the machine. This does not originate with Marx, but it is characteristic of the way Marxists have read Hegel—and it is closely related to Feuerbach's claim that we make gods in our own image. All three (Marx, Feuerbach, and Hegel) are Lutheran to the extent that they identify our god(s) as that in which we place our trust. The flip side of this is that our demons—the adversary that Christian tradition has personified in Satan—are what inspires our fear, which is marked by mistrust. Both gods and demons rise out of the works in the practice of everyday life, which feeds them. In the act of being ourselves, we make the ghosts that haunt us.

I've already suggested that, while what in the West is called dissent is the spectre with which Havel begins, it is bureaucracy in its peculiarly modern form that haunts his writing. More to the point, it is the total State that dominated the 20th century—a system that draws its power from the work of those it contains and diverges from what is usually thought of as dictatorship in being historically rooted and largely independent of the imposition of brute force. Its survival does not depend on having the largest or best equipped army so much as it depends on its reproduction by the everyday work of ordinary citizens (and hence the voluntary compliance of those citizens). This is important because it suggests that the total State can come in forms that are not limited to those of the old Soviet bloc. In fact, it suggests that "democracy" in some form may be the form best suited to it.

The particular ghost that haunts Havel leads him from what in the West is called dissent to the "dissidents" with which it is identified—from act to agent (in terms taken from Kenneth Burke's dramatistic analysis). "Who are they?" he asks—"Can they actually change anything?" That question again calls up the spectre of Marx, who said in his eleventh thesis on Feuerbach that "up to now the philosophers have only interpreted the world; the point, however, is to change it." For Havel, the question is how (or whether) a category of "subcitizens outside the power establishment" can influence the social system. What sort of power is available to those who are defined into powerlessnes? That leads him from agent to agency to scene, with purpose already in mind—to "the nature of power in the circumstances in which these powerless people operate."

Understanding the nature of power in these circumstances leads Havel to distinguish the system in which he writes (Czechoslovakia post-1968, pre-Velvet Revolution) from classical dictatorship. Classical dictatorship, he says, is historically rootless and ephemeral. It is rule by a minority clearly distinguishable from a majority, and—as already suggested—depends on armed force for its power. Havel is convinced that this is not the system in which he lives. I would carry that a step further and say that what is known as "democracy" had triumphed so thoroughly by the second half of the twentieth century that it essentially goes without saying. Power belongs to the people and the question is how to mobilize that power and keep it from getting out of hand.

Havel offers five points of distinction from classical dictatorship. First, "the system is not limited in a local, geographical sense" (evidence of the forces of dispersal that so interested Harris Stone). Second, the system does not lack historical roots. In Havel's context, the roots lie in proletarian and socialist movements of the nineteenth century. Third, the system commands a "precise, logically structured, generally comprehensible and, in a sense, extremely flexible ideology" that functions as a religion: "the center of power," Havel writes, "is identical with the centre of truth." Fourth, while exercising power in a traditional dictatorship is improvisational, it is ritualized in the system Havel describes. Fifth, while classical dictatorships are marked by "revolutionary excitement, heroism, dedication, and boisterous violence on all sides," the system Havel describes is "simply another form of the consumer and industrial society." (This last point is particularly prescient in terms of the direction "socialism with Chinese characteristics" has taken since opening and reform and especially since Tiananmen Square.) The system Havel has in mind, then, is global, historically rooted, characterized by an ideology that functions as a religion, exercises power in ways that are more ritualized than improvisational, and is a form of consumerism emerging from industrial society. Sound familiar?

It's no surprise that every second shop
on Sixth Street is some kind of mission;
but I've circled the center of this sad city
today, and I'm in no mood for a sermon
on the end of days unless it's wrapped in
a Samuel Beckett play or I'm delivering it.

So when the owner of the deli I stumble upon
comes down from the roof to unlock the door
with the big sign that led me to believe
the place was open, I look at the menu,
take note of the Bible verses on every wall,
and hope I can get out with nothing

more than coffee and small talk
about late March snow Friday.
But talking about the weather means
talking about dry, and talking about dry
means talking about prayer. I saw the sign

that said *pray for rain* when I walked in
and thought it was an invitation to something metaphorical.
But it turns out there's going to be an actual meeting,
and I suppose they won't let anyone out of the tent
until they've opened a window in the firmament
to let the water above pour in to the world

below. And once the window's open,
it's a short step from prayer
to a click of the tongue
and a knowing comment about how *they*
have laid it out this way and we're near
the end of time just living out prophecy. Today

I can't help myself and say
and who are "they"?

Well it's all there in Scripture
the owner says

and I say
what's *all there*
and who are they?

How we just have to wait
until Israel takes over
he says
and they are like
the three richest families in Amarillo
running everything here.

And I say *where do you get this stuff?*
and he says *it's all right there in Scripture*
and I say *do you read Hebrew?*
do you read Greek?
and he says *as a matter of fact*
and pulls a Strong's Concordance
out from behind the counter to show me
he has Hebrew in the house
and I say *this isn't Scripture*
and he says *it's like a dictionary*
and I say *if you're going to go off*
about what's in Scripture you ought
to take the time to study
the languages it's written in
and he says *so you've studied*
Hebrew and Greek and I tell him
a hell of a lot more than I should
if I really want to get out of here
without a sermon. He says *it's like a dictionary*
they put together when King James wrote
the King James Bible and I say *for Christ's sake*
King James didn't write the Bible. He just happened to be
the king of England when he got people who'd studied

Hebrew and Greek together to translate it
and I get up to pay for the coffee.

I've already made the mistake of mentioning Chicago
more than once and even having done time
at an Episcopal seminary
and he says *I don't know, man—*
being exposed to all those religions
is dangerous and I say *what religions?*
and he says *just different religions*
and I don't even think it's worth the effort
to try to tell him Episcopalians belong
to the same religion he does and besides
by now I'm not so sure so I say *do you ever*
talk to folks who belong to different religions?
Do you ever listen? Do a lot of Muslims come in
here? Buddhists? He says *they pretty much keep to themselves*

and I guess now I know who "they" are. I say *I think*
you ought to try to talk with folks and have
a serious conversation whenever you can
and he starts spouting numbers
that mark verses in Galatians
and says *we're living in the end of days*
waiting for God to come and I think
maybe this is Beckett after all and want to say
think, Lucky, think and sing *the dog went in the kitchen*
but talk instead about how we're fighting
two wars we shouldn't be fighting
and the crowd of men waiting
on Adams at the day labor place
for a few crappy jobs and how we might
try doing something about that
and he says *what do you suggest?*

and I say *Micah had it just about right:*
do justice love kindness walk humbly
with your god and he says
where does the "do" come from?
and I say *Jesus Christ* out loud
while I dig out two dollars
and tell him to keep the change
and he might think for a moment
he's converted me but then he realizes
I was swearing not answering
my own question and he says *I'm sorry*
we don't see eye to eye and I say *I'm not sorry*
about that at all, but I am sorry we can't have
a serious conversation and he says *have a blest day*
and I say *peace* and *I hope your business thrives*
while you're waiting for the end of the world
and he locks up and I get back on the road
wondering what in heaven's name he's doing
on the roof with the door locked behind a sign
that says *we're open, come in.*

III

¶ It is at this point that Havel returns to the greengrocer mentioned earlier, the one who places the slogan *Workers of the world unite!* in his shop window. Havel doesn't object to the semantic content of the sign, but he believes it is largely irrelevant to the shopkeeper, who puts the sign in the window not because he believes it but because it's "been done that way for years, because everyone does it, and because that is the way it has to be." The "real meaning" of the slogan reflects the greengrocers "vital interests," which Havel connects with ideology. The sign allows the greengrocer "to conceal from himself the low foundations of his obedience" while also concealing "the low foundations of power." Ideology is the "high" facade behind which they are hidden. Havel calls ideology a "specious" way of relating to the world—directed to God and to humankind as a way to conceal one's real *modus vivendi* from oneself and the world.

One of my teachers—Juan Luis Segundo—was more charitable in his definition of ideology, which he considered to be a system of efficacy (as opposed to faith, by which he meant "a world of meaning and value"). Both Havel and Segundo are rooted in Marx, and both are rooted in Husserl (Segundo by way of Ricoeur, Havel by way of Patočka)—so it is worth reminding ourselves that what is "high" is built on what is low, often in such a way as to conceal it. Superstructure is high; base is low—but base is what you must get to if you want to understand power.

Ideology and faith are both superstructure in Segundo (one does not arise from the other, though both arise from the same source). A single ideology may be compatible with multiple faiths, and vice versa. Havel and Segundo intersect on the question of what happens when faith and ideology come into conflict. Havel's point (in Segundo's terms) is that, given the distortion of ideology in Czechoslovakia between Prague Spring and the Velvet Revolution, you must change your ideology or it will change your faith. (This, by the way, is Ivan Jirous's "second culture.")

Havel's identification with Charter 77 and the human rights movement introduces the question of "universals" at exactly this point—in Segundo's terms, is there a "universal" faith, equivalent to Havel's "living in truth"? "Between the aims of the post-totalitarian system and the aims of life," Havel writes, "there is a yawning abyss..."

Ideology begins as an instrument of power—a system of efficacy—but the roles are reversed as systems become "total": power comes to serve ideology. Havel refers to "the dictatorship of the ritual," which he says renders power anonymous. Stone's *Dispersed City* takes a similar turn—in Barry Newton's words, "Faced with the reality of dispersal, it promotes the critical work of making lives and ideas within the settings of proprietorial anonymity. One of the required actions is the remaking of abandoned structures; the second the remaking of ideas."

People are unaware of the slogan on the placard in the greengrocer's window, but they are very much aware of "the panorama of everyday life," which reminds them where they are and what is expected of them: what drops out of sight is most critical. Havel describes the internalization of class struggle—not a social order imposed by one group on another but something that permeates the whole. This internalization is reminiscent of Marcuse and extends Hegel's analysis of slave consciousness and the master/slave relationship in a consistently Marxist fashion. The most oppressive system is the one that most consistently internalizes oppression. The more perfectly it is internalized, the more unnecessary is the application of external power. A system that succeeded in perfectly internalizing oppression would be a system in which the oppressed consistently believed themselves to be free while choosing their own oppression. What makes this most significant if we want to think critically about power is that it directs our attention to cracks and fissures in what appears to be a seamless system—the more seamless, the more difficult to find openings. Havel, Benda, Jirous (and the Plastic People of the Universe) all point to artists as key players in exposing the cracks. This is consistent with Brecht (*art is not a mirror with which to reflect reality but a hammer with which to shape it*)—but not identical. Havel is not overtly political in his art (nor are the Plastic People of the

Universe), but documenting the absurdity of the system has political significance in that it exposes the edges (like pulling aside the curtain that hides the wizard).

This calls to mind Foucault's assertion that power comes from everywhere (as distinct from Mao's *power comes from the barrel of a gun*). But it also calls to my mind A.G. Mojtabai's response to Mao's comment (cited by Paulo Freire) that "we give back to the masses clearly what we have received from them confusedly." She wrote this response in an inscription in one of her novels, *A Stopping Place*: "my task is to document the confusion—a necessary, if limited, first step."

Havel characterizes the ritual context in which we live, "consumerism that emerges from industrial society," as living a lie. I say *we* because, while Havel was a relentless critic of the Stalinist state imposed on Czechoslovakia in the aftermath of the second world war and reimposed after Prague Spring—relentless enough to finally abandon the term "socialist" in describing his own thought, in spite of his Marxist analysis and his admiration for those involved in the nineteenth century popular movements Stalinism coopted—he was equally unwavering in his insistence that living a lie was not simply a function of the Stalinist state. The ritual context in which we live is one in which we do almost everything we do because we believe that is the way it is done here—and every time we do it that way, we strengthen the perception that this is the way it is done. We are the greengrocer, convinced, it seems, that this place we inhabit in relative peace will disappear if we do otherwise, and it sometimes seems the context has been constructed with such perfect opacity that we cannot see what lies beneath the signs of our habitual obedience.

It seems to me that we do not occupy this ritual context so much as we are occupied by it.

Havel was optimistic in the way Martin Luther King was optimistic: *the arc of the universe is long, but it is toward justice.* Havel's version is focused on a predilection to truth, which renders a system based on living a lie unstable. This is especially interesting against the background of phenomenology. Is there a clear distinction between appearance and reality? Havel sometimes speaks as though the answer is yes—but I think we are on more solid ground if we acknowledge that what we have is always a clash of interpretations. It is not appearance versus reality but appearance versus appearance. And in this world of infinite mirrors, we struggle to make our way humanly.

Havel's response to living a lie is breathtakingly simple: live in truth.

The "heroic" consists in being fully human here, now. What is most striking to me about the Plastic People of the Universe and Havel is that, even though Havel did "go to the castle," they consistently thumbed their noses at the popular tendency (ridiculed by e.e. cummings in one of my favorite poems from his 1950 collection Χαιρε) to make a hero of any jerk afraid to answer "no."

Heidegger famously said "a god is the only thing that can save us now"— and that, I think, goes a long way toward explaining his predilection to fascism. Albert Camus offered a pithy rejoinder when he suggested that "to kill god and to build a church are the constant and contradictory purpose of rebellion."

From one table over in a coffee shop in Columbia, Missouri, in September 2012 (a few days after yom kippur) in the middle of what sounded like a long and intense conversation between two young men interested in Christianity and politics, I overheard one say: "You mean the United States attacked Libya?" That shock in a college town between two students is indicative of the extent to

which our military machine "goes without saying": it is as
invisible as the placard in the greengrocer's window.

> *The sound of gunfire, off in the distance,*
> *I'm getting used to it now*
> *Lived in a brownstone, lived in the ghetto,*
> *I've lived all over this town*
> *—Talking Heads*

I know I know Shaman's Sage grows elsewhere
in the Sierra Madre de Oaxaca, no doubt
closer to heaven. But here salvia

everywhere is divine
in spring, and, seeing all
these cousins, I see things every time.

North, quiet, no sign of an occupation
today. Purple clematis clings
to an iron fence. There is

an occasional flag, an uprising
now and then, but nothing like the field of them
year after year on my granny's half acre.

Mansions of the sort
the leaders of the occupation
gathered here for a weekend must inhabit,

far from the street behind iron gates.
Signs warn passersby not
to loiter, not to cross the line.

A mosque and a BP station face off
like guard towers, each at a corner
of an imagined world.

Mansions turn to row houses,
row houses to apartments
that must be section 8,

then elegant old homes
boarded up now
and a field of weeds for sale.

The next sign the city is occupied is
a helicopter brooding over the face of the water
at the tomb of Stephen Douglas, the spirit, they say,

of a middle way on slavery, evolving. There is
yellow tape across the path to mark a police line
just beyond Soldier Field, just beyond the simple marker

that says *a riot is the language of the unheard*
near the spot where there was a race riot in 1919,
which I suppose could have been placed at random

in this country. Iron and steel fences
have been erected around a museum
draped with Genghis Khan's face,

gates ready to slam
if things get out of hand.
Two blocks of snow plows

on the sidewalk at Balbo,
mobile barricades
I suppose.

A crowd in Daley Plaza, around Picasso's old baboon,
smirking as he always does, no larger than the one
at Wrigley today for crosstown baseball.

Bob Marley sings "Stand Up," Beatles "Can't Buy Me
Love" while people in Robin Hood hats looking
for all the world like elves dance.

People take signs they did not make
with slogans they did not think
to wave for cameras everywhere.

Chicago cops cluster at the corners,
a line of state troopers behind barricades
on the north, between the crowd

and the city's seat of power.
One person after another stops
to take a photo of the line of troopers,

who have an official photographer
to take photos of every one
who takes photos.

Every other
step disrupts
somebody's photo op.

Someone talking on a cellphone passes,
saying *what are you guys protesting about?*
A trooper marches by with a cluster of plastic restraints

clipped to his belt...
reminds me of the line of old buses
I passed earlier at McCormick Place, empty,

waiting for detainees to move away from here.
Pigeons are frantic. This crowd may be as generous
as the everyday, but there are fewer orts and fragments

a pigeon might be inclined to consume.
After an hour, I walk to Monks,
consider my options.

The server says *you want Revolution,*
and I say *damn right*. She
brings two

with grilled cheese
and sweet potato fries,
and I believe that has done

as much to change the world
as the long walk on the lake
and standing anonymous

in a crowd that is most surprising for nothing
if not how much it looks like business
as usual.

FIVE
A Song of Freedom:
Reinventing the Franciscan Revolution

¶It is customary in delivering a lecture to reserve foot-notes for the written version, which often appears after the fact (as is the case with this one), with notes at the end. Since this lecture lies somewhere on the spectrum between a long poem and a sermon, what is customary is probably not of central importance—and my custom, in any case, is to back into scholarly matters the way a short-stop backs into shallow left field to reach a blooper before it drops for a hit. (I know baseball metaphors are painful in early October in Chicago this year. But scholarly publishing being what it is, the White Sox could be on their way to another World Series by the time this is published, so I hope you'll bear with me.)

In any case, backing into this, I begin with four notes. There may be more in the published version.

1. The reader is advised never to trust a poem or a joke (not to mention a sermon) with footnotes.

2. Emma Goldman also said she had no time to write the story of her life because she was busy living it. She said this in a memoir that comes to almost a thousand pages in the edition I have on my bookshelf. Surely you can under-stand why what she said isn't necessarily suited to a t-shirt.

3. One of the most revolutionary things about language is that no word ever means one thing.

4. I'm telling you now, as laozi said: "Cats that know don't tell. Cats that tell don't know." (See *daodejing 56*.)

I

One of the paradoxes of being
left in the United States is
there is no there there
for a party. We
all know Red Emma

almost said *if I can't dance, I*
don't want to join your revolution,
by which I think she meant to say
What's a revolution without a dance?—
not a question but a party platform.

(It may have been Rosa. But
a rose by any other, as
the saying goes,
is a rose is
a rose
is a rose).

And the dance is
another story.

Climb one more,
Wang Zhihuan said, to see
another thousand li.

One can climb down
as well as up, and climbing down
(as any cat who's ever been stuck up
a tree can tell you) is
the hard part.

When Whitehead said
Western philosophy is a footnote
to Plato, he had his eye on climbing
down. You know the old story
about a chance encounter
between philosophers
on the way home
from a religious festival

in honor of a moon
goddess—

a hunter, they say,
always in the middle
of a dance—it begins
along the lines of *a priest
and a rabbi went into a bar...*
and one thing leads to another.

Before you know it, Plato
has a circle of friends spinning
a city in the clouds; and we
are still making our way
to the bottom of it.

A footnote to Plato is
a footnote to a footnote to
a footnote dancing
around justice,
among other things.

And that means thinking
through (if not speaking truth
to) power.

II

¶ In July 1294, three eminent dignitaries, a bunch of monks,
and a crowd climbed a mountain...

As far as I know, there is no record of Pietro the hermit
saying *is this some kind of joke?* when they informed him he
had been chosen pope. But why not? If you climbed the
highest mountain you knew hoping to see to the bottom

of things in time, with solitude, what would *you* say if a crowd showed up and told you you'd been elected pope?

It was a story about seeing things that got Pietro noticed.

One version of the story puts the fear of God in a college of cardinals squabbling over politics, and the rest is history. Pietro took the job, changed his name to protect the innocent, and, after a short interval, resigned.

Resignation—*that* resignation—is a critical footnote in the history of the West, closely connected to an Augustinian reading of Plato that underwrites his admonition (in a reading of an epistle of John) to love and do what you will.

Technically, Celestine V was not a disciple of Francis. He was a Benedictine (which makes it likely that the party that climbed the mountain to find him was offered a drink even if we didn't get the part of the old joke about walking into a bar).

Strictly speaking, though, Celestine's story is among the most likely with which to flesh out Franciscan spirituality.

In the history of the papacy, it is generally seen to be a disaster. And yet Celestine was declared a saint (the patron of bookbinders, mind you) within two decades of his death.

III

My teacher Richard Luecke used to say
the powers that be (god knows who
god knows where he added with
a wink if the context
called for it)

deal with rabble rousers in three ways:
Declare them criminals and keep them in jails.

Declare them insane and keep them in asylums.
Declare them saints and keep them in churches.

By some accounts, Celestine was a triple threat.

IV

¶Before he was Celestine, Pietro founded a particularly strict community of Benedictine monks that became known as Celestines after his election as pope. In the beginning, the community had no written rule but followed what had drawn them together, Pietro's own practice as a hermit—a *Benedictine* hermit. When Urban IV confirmed the order, he made the Rule of Saint Benedict their guide.

As a hermit, Celestine was not alone in drawing a crowd. He took John the Baptist as model, and, like his model, he was surrounded by a growing body of devoted followers. A *practice* of withdrawal around which a crowd gathers is a public thing that calls for politics (which transforms the crowd into a city, a story Pietro would have known from the desert fathers, for whom the *desert* was a city). In the Benedictine tradition, the moment between the crowd and the city is mediated by the practice of hospitality, in which interruptions become one's life.

Pietro's election as pope is one such interruption.

Such moments are placed in a rhythm of work in which work is prayer (without ceasing, as Paul put it). The work of the community transforms the world the way prayer does (which, of course, raises the question of how prayer transforms the world), and that way has been at the heart of the dance in Augustinian communities (as in the Platonic depiction of the Socratic community as a moveable feast well aware of the power of song).

A community that understands its work as prayer and

in which hospitality governs interaction with strangers and guests is by necessity improvisational, marked by a rhythm that is determined both by the ordinary time of work (the daily office) and the extraordinary encounter with strangers whose presence means a new (unexpected) order that reorients the work of the community as hospitality and redefines the stranger as guest.

This has sometimes been seen as a radically different reading than that of Plato's student Aristotle in the two volume work we know as *Politics* and *Nicomachean Ethics*. But I see a clear family resemblance in the two readings in their attention to *friendship*, which always raises the radical ethical question of what we mean by "we" and calls attention to the dance on the edges where friends encounter strangers. That dance and those edges shape every human city.

There is also a family resemblance in the attention to the closely related edges defined by the encounter of freedom with necessity, which, like the hermit who is not alone, embodies a paradox of human existence.

One way of naming that paradox is to say the *we* is that by which *I* am. Another (which, in the end, comes to the same thing) is the paradox with which Luther begins his treatise on the freedom of the Christian: "*Ein Christenmensch ist ein freier Herr über alle Dinge und niemand untertan. Ein Christenmensch ist ein dienstbarer Knecht aller Dinge und jedermann untertan*". ["A Christian person is a free lord over all things and subject to no one. A Christian person is a dutiful servant of all things and subject to everyone."]

I read the second assertion in Luther's paradox as a radically Franciscan statement of the experience of necessity in human existence. I am going to take the liberty of replacing Luther's *Christenmensch* with *mensch* so that the second assertion reads *a mensch is a dutiful servant of all things and subject to everyone.* The second part of the second part personalizes it by saying the *mensch* is subject to everyone. That has interesting ethical implications to which I will return, but, for the moment, I am more interested in the first part of the second part, which makes the *mensch* "a dutiful servant of all things." There is a necessity in human existence that arises from our mutual subjection in community: the fact that there is a *we* (and the corollary *they*) means that my freedom is conditioned by wills other than my own. But there is a more radical necessity that derives from our connectedness to all things, stated here in a radical form that goes beyond simple connectedness: to be fully human is not only to be connected to all things but also to be at the service of all things. It is this radical statement of radical necessity that leads me to characterize Luther's paradox as Franciscan.

For Luther as for Francis (both drinking from the same Augustinian well) that necessity is unavoidably incarnational (a particularly interesting footnote that repudiates disembodied readings of Plato such as that, for example, of Plotinus).

In Franciscan spirituality, this goes well beyond the simile that often follows an analogical reading: be like Jesus (in contemporary parlance, an imperative masquerading as a question in the acronym WWJD). The appearance of the stigmata is an unmistakable metaphor: Francis (like Jesus) *is* Christ crucified. And Luther makes it plain in his treatise that we are to be Christs (not Christ impersonators) to one another.

This spin on the Augustinian tradition reaches back to "Eastern" sources (notably Origen) that have been far more comfortable with *theosis*—divinization—than the "Western" church. In Luther's treatise, the analogical reading and its accompanying simile is a kind of *hubris*, implying that in our work we can do what Jesus did. Luther criticized this "works righteousness" and maintained instead that we become Christs by grace through faith. We become Christs not by the power of our will but by the infinite resignation of faith (not an action but a passion). That infinite resignation transforms our work and frees us to be who we are.

With another noted hermit in the "Western" tradition, I turn farther east, to Zhuangzi, for an illustration of this transformed work in the person of Cook Ding:

Cook Ding is chopping an ox for Wen Huijun,

hand touches,
shoulder leans,
foot steps,
knee bends,
thus and thus,
thus plays the knife,
working together in time.

dancing "The Mulberry Grove" together, an ensemble playing "Jing Shou." Wen Huijun says "Whee! Wonderful! How can skill reach such heights?" Cook Ding puts down the knife and says: "Minister, what I care about is dao, something beyond skill. When I began cutting up oxen, I saw nothing but the ox. After three years, I no longer saw the whole ox. Today I use the spirit to encounter it and not the eye. The official knows when to stop, the spirit when to go on. In accordance with heaven's structure, I cut along the main seams, follow the natural course.

It is interesting that perhaps the most familiar (though not necessarily the best known) hermit in the United States,

Henry David Thoreau, also turns east, to the *Bhagavadgi-ta*, which describes the *mensch* (in the voice of Krishna, as "transcreated" by P. Lal) as the one *who dares to see action in inaction and inaction in action*. Which leads to a little more on Cook Ding:

dancing with his hands, Butcher Ding says

*When I began, I saw
nothing but the ox.*

*After three years,
I saw no ox.*

*Now I cut eyes closed,
follow what is, see nothing.*

*A good cook changes knives once a year.
A bad cook changes knives month in,
month out. Nineteen years*

*and my knife is good as new.
Spaces between joints, no*

*thickness to the edge of the blade,
there is room for play. When*

*I come to a hard place, I go slow
until the whole falls apart like a clod of dirt*

*crumbling. Satisfied,
I stand. I have no desire*

to go on.

Plato, Cook Ding, and, I might add, my late father, agree that one should divide at the joints. I have no idea what kind of butcher Plato was (though he was speaking in the voice of Socrates, so the question, I suppose, is what kind of butcher Plato imagined Socrates to be). Cook Ding's skill is legendary (though, if Zhuangzi is to be believed, he denied that it was skill). I know my father, who told me this while he was cutting up a chicken for frying, could do it, as they say, with his eyes closed—the way Zhuangzi would have us believe Cook Ding could butcher an ox.

V

¶The party line is that Celestine V abdicated because he did not have the administrative skills necessary to be pope—in short, because he was not up to the job. But what if we read his brief papacy, the acceptance of the election together with the abdication—in the light of his support for the Spiritual Franciscans, as a single act of resignation? What if we read it not as a simile but as a metaphor in the spirit of Hosea?

To refresh your memory, Hosea is the minor prophet God ordered to marry an unfaithful woman to demonstrate the relationship between God and Israel. For now, we'll pass over questions about the role of prophet, the meaning of prophecy, and the significance of claims to receive orders from God. What we won't pass over is the *structure*: Hosea acts in such a way as to embody the relationship between God and the people of God. What would it mean if Celestine saw himself doing something along these lines?

We might also take note of the fact that the previous Celestine (Celestine IV, who died in 1241) was pope for 17 days. Celestine II (who died in 1144) was pope for five months. (There was also an antipope Celestine II for one day—16 December 1124.) The first Celestine (who died in 432) was an outspoken opponent of the Pelagians, and Celestine III (who died in 1198) is said to have been ready to resign before he died but was prevented from doing so.

With all due respect to Dante, Celestine's abdication bears the marks not of a *refusal* motivated by cowardice (which would have enabled Pietro to stay on the mountaintop, where we have every reason to believe he would have prefered to stay) but of a *repudiation* (which required him to climb down and become pope—though it didn't require him to keep the job for long). It is an interesting inversion of the yes and no of Camus' rebel—not resisting power externally imposed but embracing such power in order to let it go, an act that (quite apart from whether it "worked") shook Rome to its foundations well before the "Protestant" reformation by reiterating the question Francis raised with his radical embrace of poverty.

VI

¶ That question, which cuts to the heart of the matter in much the same way Plato's justice among other things does, was what *is* the Church?

At a time when many are ready to throw the baby of corporate personhood out with the bathwater of entrenched campaign finance practices that have made the United States a plutocracy, much of the discussion of that matter looks markedly anachronistic. But if a lecture series under the aegis of the Basic Program doesn't provide a place for discussion marked anachronistic, I fear such discussion has no place. And that would impoverish our politics both philosophically and spiritually. So let us sin boldly.

VII

¶I won't presume to enter into the mind of the pope or the mysteries of the magisterium; but, whether or not Benedict XVI and Francis I actively conspired to turn our minds to Celestine V, Francis of Assisi, and the politics of abdication, that is effectively what they did. And, between them, I believe they effected the most significant theological work of Joseph Ratzinger's long career.

Their corporate act contained the theological/ecclesiological possibility that prompted then Cardinal Ratzinger to silence the Franciscan Leonardo Boff for a year after the publication of his *Igreja: Carisma e poder* (*Church: Charism and Power*) in 1981.

Containing the theological/ecclesiological possibility was probably exactly what Ratzinger had in mind when Boff was officially silenced in 1985 (the year the book appeared in English). If so, the abdication of Benedict—together with the new pope taking the name of Francis—may be read as the second act, completing the first.

A possibility contained in an act of theology is a cat in a box like the one Erwin Schrödinger imagined: it collapses, dead or alive, only under the gaze of the physicist (or the Inquisitor) who demands certainty.

Which means *containing* the possibility—intended to keep it from getting out of hand—may bring to mind a possible cat in a possible box that would make Saint Francis smile.

I read this against the background of the argument Boff made in *Church: Charism and Power*, the Vatican's response to that argument (orchestrated by the Sacred Congregation for the Doctrine of the Faith, of which Ratzinger was prefect at the time), and the later dispute between Leonardo Boff and his brother Clodovis (with whom he wrote an introduction to liberation theology published in Portuguese in 1986 and in English a year later).

The argument hinges on the ecclesiological claim—which reaches back beyond Augustine to Paul—that the Church is the body of Christ and the question of where this body stands in relation to the poor. Bear in mind that the fuss surrounding the Franciscan order that began even before Francis died was almost entirely about his unequivocal embrace of poverty (and particularly his embrace of poverty in the rule written to govern the order he founded). The spiritual Franciscans who left the order under fire and came to be identified first as Celestines then as Fraticelli insisted that the embrace not be qualified, and they had the *Testament* of Saint Francis to support them.

That the embrace (like economics in general) has more to do with power than with money is borne out by the long history of attempts to clarify a simple rule whose author wrote that he did not want it in the hands of professional clarifiers in the academy or the Church.

VIII

¶For Boff, as for other liberation theologians, theology (including ecclesiology) is the *second* step. The first step is *practice*. So *Church: Charism and Power* begins with a description of practice. That practice takes place in the world, which is the scene of God's action: it goes without saying that God is present in the world. The Church is *not* that presence: it is a sign, an instrument, in which that presence is most concretely anticipated.

Boff condemns the absolutization of Church that results from its confusion with the Kingdom of God as "ecclesiolatry." The Church, he says, is not the incarnation of Christ but the incarnation of Christianity. Not God's presence in the world (because that presence cannot be contained), the Church is a part of the world that *defines* itself as present to God. And this shifts attention from a presence understood as *static* (Being itself, which must simply be acknowledged) to a presence understood as active (*human* action in the world, which demands response). Not Presence, *presencing*.

The question is how the Church understands itself and how that understanding shapes its practice. (Does it, Boff asks, act in such a way as to reveal God's presence in the world—in *human* action, which is the only kind of action of which it is capable?) He identifies four models, three inherited, one new.

First is Church as "City of God," which he identifies as a Church "turned in on itself," acting as though it believes it is, as he says, the Kingdom—the presence of God in the world.

Second is Church as *"Mater et Magistra,"* mother and teacher, a "colonial" model in which there are two hierarchies, one civil and one religious. In this model, the Church is a Church *for* the poor rather than *with* and *of* the poor. (This a critical element in the Vatican response and becomes particularly important in the later argument with Clodovis.)

Third is Church as "sacrament of salvation," God's presence is "the great rainbow beneath which are the world and the Church. The world is understood as the place of God's activity, of the building of his Kingdom here and now... The Church, then, is seen as sacrament, the sign and instrument through which Christ and his Spirit act for the realization of the Kingdom within the world in an explicit and concrete way within the Church." Boff has some sympathy for this post-Vatican II ecclesiology (an ecclesiology in which Ratzinger had a hand), but he criticizes it as reformist, as defining its relationship with the poor from the perspective of the rich.

Fourth is "a Church from the poor." This is the model of the base ecclesial community that takes the view from below or from the margin. It sees poverty and oppression as systemic problems that require systemic solutions rather than reform. Boff describes this as a process in which "initially, such a community serves to deepen the faith of its members, to prepare the liturgy, the sacraments, and the life of prayer. At a more advanced stage these members begin to help each other. As they become better organized and reflect more deeply, they come to the realization that the problems they encounter have a structural character. Their marginalization is seen as a consequence of elitist organization, private ownership, that is, of the very socioeconomic structure of the capitalist system. Thus the question of politics arises and the desire for liberation is set in a concrete and historical context. The community sees this not only as liberation from sin (from which we must always liberate ourselves) but also as liberation that has economic, political, and cultural dimensions. Christian faith directly seeks the ultimate liberation and freedom of the children of God in the Kingdom, but it also includes historical liberation as an anticipation and concretization of that ultimate liberation."

This fourth model, which he calls new (though I think it is older than the other three), goes beyond the third by making the *world* a sacrament. Christian faith acts in the world, and in that action God's presence is visible. Neither Church nor world is identified with Kingdom, but both live in the Kingdom, and the Kingdom is alive in both. "The Christian community and the political community are two open spheres where what is properly Christian circulates."

Boff describes his new model as *ecclesiogenesis*, identifying Church as process rather than product and defining the process as practical activity in the world. The question is not what the Church *is* but what it *does*.

That emphasis on practice is the revolutionary turn that precipitates containment strategies (as it did in response to Francis and his radical embrace of poverty).

Theology is a discipline undertaken in a specific historical context, in the context of the world. As such, it is intrinsically connected to historical and social problems. On the one hand, this means that every theological tendency is particular and cannot pass itself off as absolute. On the other hand, it means that the sociohistorical and political context in which theology is undertaken and to which theology addresses itself will be determinative of the perspectives it takes. Theology, because it is a historical task, is political, just as the Church, because it is in the world, is historical and political. The problem this poses for Boff is how to identify the most appropriate theological tendency for Church and society here and now.

Here, the image of Church as the incarnation of *Christianity* is especially important. He characterizes Catholicism as "a principle of the incarnation of Christianity in history," as "the mediation of Christianity." The *mediation* becomes crucial. It is "the Gospel made concrete," but it is *not* the Gospel. It is the body of Christ, but it is *not* Christ. "Given both the identity and nonidentity of the Church and the Gospel," he writes, "two styles of Christian life are possible: one enthusiastically accepts historical mediations because they make present the Gospel, Jesus, and his cause. The other will constantly criticize all mediations because it cannot see either the living Gospel or the living Christ in them; rather it sees only human constructs and so continually seeks the greater purity of the Divine."

The Church is intrinsically connected with incarnation, where he says we confront the mystery of an identity that is both revealed and hidden. This is as true of the Church as incarnation of Christianity as it is of Jesus as incarnation of God.

Boff carries this further in his discussion of syncretism, where he argues that Catholicism "implies a courage for incarnation, an acceptance of heterogeneous elements and their subsequent integration within the criteria of a specifically Catholic ethos. Catholicity as the synonym of universality is only possible and attainable through the process of syncretism from which catholicity itself results." Boff insists that Christianity, because it emerged (and continues to emerge) within a concrete historical context, brought with it (and continues to bring with it) the cultural heritage and specificity of all the individuals that come together to make it. Christianity "is a cultural product... as syncretic as any other religious expression." And syncretism is *not* "a pathology of pure religion." It is "a normal condition of the incarnation, expression, and objectification of a religious faith or expression." When a religious faith takes on historical expression, it is engaged in a syncretic process. The Church, as the incarnation of Christianity, is an example of such a process. To be truly catholic is to be open to incarnation; to be open to incarnation is to be syncretic.

As products of culture acting in history, both Jesus of Nazareth and the Church are characterized by service, which Boff calls "charism," the source of the Church's identity and of its power. It is, he says, in the Church's service, which is the activity of the Holy Spirit in and through the people of God, that the presence of the risen Christ is made known in the world. This is the incarnation of Christianity, and, by Boff's definition, it is the Church.

It is most interesting that Boff (like Francis) puts the Church in its place in response to what he sees as an abuse of power. He embraces the human institution as *sacramental* precisely because he does not want to confuse the human institution with God.

IX

¶ Luther argued in "The Freedom of a Christian" that "It is not enough, or in any sense Christian to preach the works, life, and words of Christ as historical facts, as if the knowledge of these would suffice for the conduct of life... Far less is it sufficient or Christian to say nothing at all about Christ and to teach instead the laws and the decrees of the fathers... Rather ought Christ to be preached to the end that faith in him may be established that he may not only be Christ, but be Christ for you and me, and that what is said of him and is denoted in his name may be effected in us. Luther calls on us to become Christs to one another," to "put on" our neighbors and conduct ourselves toward them as if we ourselves were in the neighbor's place. Not only recollection, but also repetition—not just memory, but real presence.

Dietrich Bonhoeffer picks up this thread in the context of the German church struggle and the ecumenical movement, defining Christ as "the man for others" and defining Christians as persons for others. The church as community has no boundaries except those imposed in her relationship with other communities. Precisely because the Church is the world *present* to God, it is set apart from the world that absents itself from God.

Hitler and the Nazi state promoted a positive philosophy that in many cases was supported by a Lutheran theology that thought in terms of orders of creation. Bonhoeffer was one of the clearest voices that confronted this with a negative philosophy that redefined orders as mandates. Bonhoeffer insisted on God's *presence* and the Church as the world's presence before God. This meant that Christians, as a community called by God, did not respond to "orders" forever fixed in the nature of things but rather to God. Like Boff, Bonhoeffer recognized that the tendency to absolutize is itself pathological. Where a particular sphere of existence takes on absolute dimensions, the political function of the church is to relativize it, to insist that it also is present to God.

Luther balanced what he referred to as the "inner" and "spiritual" aspect of human existence with an "outward" and "physical" aspect. In our spiritual aspect, we are perfectly free and do no works; but in our physical aspect, we are servants and do "all kinds of works." Our works do not justify us, but they spring "out of spontaneous love in obedience to God." Luther's understanding of "two kingdoms" is properly viewed against the backdrop of this distinction between two aspects of human existence as one God's two rules. As in Boff, the "kingdoms" appear to be concentric spheres in which one God is sovereign. As Boff suggests, the Kingdom—the one God's rule—is the source of both Church and world, and the practical activity of Christians in response to the presence of the kingdom is the source of politics and the structure of the Church.

Individual Christians reflect this in the fact that we live simultaneously in both realms. It is not one person who lives "in the world" and one who lives "in God's kingdom." One person living in the world is in God's kingdom—*simul iustus et peccator*. Our justification is God's act; our sanctification grows out of that act. Although human action in history is not the basis for salvation, it is of central importance, because God's saving act is the basis from which it grows. Luther's insight was that the basis is *present* and that it makes Christians *free*. Sanctification, which proceeds on the basis of that freedom as action in history, is *political* action.

Boff's fourth model of the Church, the "new" model which he sees as being most adequate, presents the world as sacrament—or, more precisely, socio-political liberation as sacramental action. Sacramental action is action in which the world is made present to God—and the Church is human beings being human in the world, nothing more.

X

¶I am not going to recount the Vatican response to Boff's book line by line. That is partly because there is not time and partly because, much as I have disagreed with Joseph Ratzinger's positions over the years, I have never questioned the clarity of his theological reasoning. He was the primary author of the response, so I direct you to the source.

Suffice it to say that Ratzinger's strategy was very similar to that his predecessors used in dealing with Francis. They chose their targets carefully, isolated the radicals, and qualified the embrace of poverty. Ratzinger qualified the embrace of liberation. Doing that as he did from a position of power and privilege fueled the arguments of "radicals" like Boff who embraced the post-Vatican II Church but criticized it for defining its relationship with the poor from the perspective of the rich. Fueling the argument drove Boff out of the Catholic Church and the Franciscan order (much as the Spiritual Franciscans were driven out of the Church and out of the order). It is interesting that driving the spirituals out of the Catholic Church and out of the Franciscan Order probably helped pave the way for the Protestant Reformation—especially its radical wing as represented by thinkers like Thomas Müntzer.

The argument that developed between Clodovis and Leonardo Boff is an important variation on this theme. Clodovis has not left the Church, and he has criticized liberation theology (most forcefully in an article published in Portuguese in 2008—in a Franciscan journal) for beginning with the poor and arriving at Christ rather than beginning with Christ and arriving at the poor. Leonardo's response is that beginning with Christ means beginning with the poor, because that's where Christ is.

Clodovis sees it as a matter of direction, consistent with the transformation of the Franciscan order into an order of service to the poor. Leonardo sees that as a strategy of containment, defining the poor from another perspective, that of the rich. Like the spiritual Franciscans, he demands a radical embrace of poverty. That, he says, is where we start—and, yes, he says, it is political.

The point, as another important Augustinian put it in the mid-19th century, is not merely to interpret the world but to change it.

XI

¶No doubt, many of you were aware of Gertrude Stein haunting the place at the beginning of this talk. She shows up in my work whenever I need to be reminded of the power of word play—attending, as she does, to the physicality of the things, their embodiment, rather than their use as vehicles. Her rose is a rose is a rose makes us think another name might not smell as sweet or feel as good on our tongues. And it reminds us that we are in conversation not only with Shakespeare but also with a controversy about names that engulfed many scholastically inclined followers of Francis (which in turn calls to mind Umberto Eco's *Name of the Rose*, which ends with *stat rosa pristina nomine, nomina nuda tenemus*).

At times we call on a name. At times we take a name to stake a claim. We name names, and sometimes we grope for a name when we have reason to believe we should recognize someone we cannot place. Calling a demon by name is one way to deprive it of its power.

A naked name is not a rose, nor is the first rose if it is a rose in name only now.

What was so troubling about the abdication of Celestine (and threatening enough to those who wanted him gone to lead them to imprison him after the fact) was that he had used the power of the papacy to relinquish power. The act had to be managed, but managing it was, for the powers that be, like herding cats.

What is so interesting about the resignation of Benedict is that a pope who had not hesitated to use his power to silence voices he thought dangerous when he was the prefect of the office previously known as the Inquisition used Celestine's precedent to draw a line around it—to show its limits.

That language of limits is, it seems to me, exactly what Saint Francis sought. And to the extent that it places the power of the papacy in the hands of the magisterium (where some would say it resided all along), it has the potential to reconstruct the Church along lines proposed by Vatican II. That is, at least, an interesting move for Benedict to make.

On the other hand, when a Jesuit assumes the papacy and takes the name of Francis, telling us not to think of Xavier is a bit like telling us not to think of a purple elephant. Names carry stories, and there is power in that.

That is why we so often take great care (or wish we had) in naming names.

I think Francis was a spectacular choice of names for the new pope, because—with one word—it focuses attention on two ways in which the Church has wielded its considerable power as a body politic. I take Leonardo's cautious statement that election of Francis is a positive sign as a gentle reminder that it might be best for this possible cat if we leave the lid on the box for now.

That calls for an abdication of certainty, an ecclesiology in which the Church becomes what it is nowhere other than in the world.

XII

¶ One more thing—not a conclusion, but a place to stop for now. It is no small thing for a people of the book to name a patron saint of those who bind them. There is a history of religion (which is itself a binding) in this, recapitulated perhaps in what is being said now about the future of the book. There are those who have no doubt the book is one thing that must be preserved in its familiar form. Binding it becomes a kind of taxidermy for the cat whose wave state has collapsed for the sake of certainty. Others know there is no end of the making of books, and for them binding is a discipline equally concerned with their power to unbind, a discipline that makes it possible to keep them opening.

I leave you with a poem inspired by *Qing dai di xizi hui* (associations for treasuring written characters of the Qing dynasty). One of the things these associations did was ritual burning of paper with writing on it–an act of reverence akin to burning a flag when it is worn out.

Every letter must burn before a god
can take it in. Nothing binds
words in books. Libraries
blaze. Breathe. Conspire.

SIX

Everything Out of Its Place:
The Work of Poetry

¶ I begin with two observations drawn from Robert Frost's prose, which consists almost entirely of correspondence and occasional pieces—writing that most clearly happens between particular people in particular places at particular times:

First, he was not interested in making the world "better." And, second, he defined poetry as "word made deed."

On first glance, these may appear to be contradictory. Insisting that he had no interest in making the world better could be taken as a repudiation of action. But the definition of poetry as word made deed is clearly a declaration that, as a poet, he is engaged—in the act of making the word deed and (presumably) the doing of the deed itself.

On closer examination, what we encounter in these two observations is a *tension* that is critical to poetry as Frost practiced it.

Poetry, Frost said, is an extravagance of grief, while politics is an extravagance of grievance. Calling poetry an extravagance of grief puts to rest any notion that Frost is simply satisfied with the world as it is. That kind of satisfaction would not inspire grief, let alone an extravagance of it. An extravagance of grief is not a sign of complacency. It identifies the particular deed of poetry, the transformation of the word effected in the act of making it, as mourning. And it does not deny the possibility that the transformation of the word effected in the mourning of poetry might also be a transformation of the world—only that the *purpose* of poetry (at least as Frost practices it) is not to make the world better. (If poetry's being in the world makes the world better, that is a side effect, not a goal.)

Frost's focus on the *extravagances* of poetry and politics, and his drawing of a line between the two, is an intriguing way to connect them: they are both extravagances (which is not the same thing as saying they are luxuries)—and they are both matters of language, one articulate and instrumental (the stuff manifestos are made of), the other (perhaps) inarticulate, an end in itself. Grief is not a demand. It is a cry, and, as Adorno said of music, it "resembles language in the sense that it is a temporal sequence of articulated sounds which are more than just sounds. They say something, often something human... The succession of sounds is like logic: it can be right or wrong. But what has been said cannot be detached from the music..."

Frost is not interested in making the world better, but he is interested in making it. And that, I think, is why Joan Richardson counts him among the founders of American pragmatism. Frost went to Harvard at least in part because that is where William James was. But James was away while he was there (as he says) waiting for him. And, as a result, he studied with Santayana. It would be hard to imagine a more fitting way for a philosopher of pragmatism to approach a promising student than by being absent. Frost learned pragmatism by not studying with William James just as James learned philosophy by not taking philosophy classes. (As he put it, the first philosophy class he ever attended was the first one he taught.)

This gives us an important clue as to how pragmatism works and, more importantly for our purposes here, how Frost's poetry works. One does not argue with grief, certainly not an extravagance of it (as one might argue with a grievance). An extravagance of grievance calls for satisfaction or denial. What can one do upon encountering an extravagance of grief but hear it? The fact of feeling, Richardson calls it by way of defining *pragma*. But the fact is a moment in the act (a perching, James might say, in flight)—the completion of an act for now, but never forever. And so it does not give us a manifesto, but it draws us in—or, viewed from our side, out, out of place, out of our place into the place of the other, grieving—which is neither here nor there. The manifesto takes a stand and challenges us to do the same: *hier stehe ich*. Grief sweeps us off our feet: it is a passion that does not demand words or action but invites compassion (putting the accent on *ich kann nicht anders*).

Let's withhold judgement for now on whether either makes the world better. The question is not what makes it better but what makes it work. What is it up to?

That is the question Frost brings to poetry—not what does it mean or what does it say but what is it up to.

And, because that is a question best answered in particular, I turn to a close reading of four of Frost's poems—"Mending Wall," "The Mountain," "A Servant to Servants," and "Christmas Trees," from his second and third collections, *North of Boston* and *Mountain Interval*. Frost says the first of those poems, "'Mending Wall,' takes up the theme where 'The Tuft of Flowers' in *A Boy's Will* laid it down." So I begin with "The Tuft of Flowers," laying down a theme, making a total of five and sampling the first three collections of Frost's poetry, published a century ago.

"The Tuft of Flowers" is effectively three sonnets broken across twenty-one rhyming couplets. When sonnets work, they *turn*, and Frost makes hay of that, letting these three fall across the swinging rhythm—aural and visual—of the paired lines. There is more turning here than grass—and it's not a stretch to think the turning serves a similar purpose. Grass cut in dew left unturned will rot before it can make hay; so someone has to follow the mower and turn it to dry in the sun. It is a solitary task, but it is a task for two.

> I went to turn the grass once after one
> Who mowed it in the dew before the sun.

The dew was gone that made the blade so keen
Before I came to view the levelled scene.

I looked for him behind an isle of trees;
I listened for his whetstone on the breeze.

But he had gone his way, the grass all mown,
And I must be, as he had been, alone,

Traditionally, we look for the turn of the sonnet after the eighth line:

"As all must be," I said within my heart,
"Whether they work together or apart."

But as I said it, swift there passed me by
On noiseless wing a 'wildered butterfly,

True to form, Frost turns in the ninth line to internal dialogue in the heart of the narrator (which we hear even though it is not spoken because we see it here—something for those who call poets "spoken word artists" to consider). But rules are made to be broken, and the better we know them the more likely they are (as Frost would put it) to bring out the mischief in us. And so a butterfly appears to turn the turn and turn us with it.

This poem comes decades before the strange attractor Edward Lorenz identified when he was working on predicting the weather (something a farmer like Frost can appreciate) came to be widely known as the butterfly curve while the science of chaos it inspired crept into popular consciousness. But if you have a butterfly in Tokyo in mind when the one in this poem appears, it will add a layer that might just enrich the reading. And since we are eavesdropping here on an unspoken monologue, it can't hurt to think of the butterfly on Zhuangzi's mind when he found himself wondering who is dreamer who is dreamed.

And the last two lines of the first fourteen in this poem, a seventh rhyming couplet, look more like a perch than a resolution:

Seeking with memories grown dim o'er night
Some resting flower of yesterday's delight.

Making hay, the I of the poem turned in to his heart—and presumably our eyes on it turned us as well. And now the butterfly in the poem but out of the heart has us following along seeking a resting flower yesterday. (I suspect I'm not the only one hearing Paul McCartney, which gives the poem a turn the poet could not anticipate.

A note to Adorno: music—whether we know it or not—resembles language in the way pieces of it draw us in time through memory to other pieces we know.)

Turning and turning again, the poem goes on:

And once I marked his flight go round and round,
As where some flower lay withering on the ground.

And then he flew as far as eye could see,
And then on tremulous wing came back to me.

I thought of questions that have no reply,
And would have turned to toss the grass to dry;

But he turned first, and led my eye to look
At a tall tuft of flowers beside a brook.

Is it just me, or has the mind of the butterfly caught the eye of the narrator so completely that he is making hay by not turning grass? Daniel Berrigan quotes the Buddha as saying "Don't just do something. Stand there."

A leaping tongue of bloom the scythe had spared
Beside a reedy brook the scythe had bared.

I left my place to know them by their name,
Finding them butterfly weed when I came.

The narrator knows a name and finds a weed—an I out of place knows a flower out of place. Do you see what I'm saying?

And then a resolution, a couplet with no full stop:

The mower in the dew had loved them thus,
By leaving them to flourish, not for us,

No full stop, so the third sonnet begins in the middle. Don't they all?

Nor yet to draw one thought of ours to him.
But from sheer morning gladness at the brim.

The butterfly and I had lit upon,
Nevertheless, a message from the dawn,

That made me hear the wakening birds around,
And hear his long scythe whispering to the ground,

And feel a spirit kindred to my own;
So that henceforth I worked no more alone;

But glad with him, I worked as with his aid,
And weary, sought at noon with him the shade;

And dreaming, as it were, held brotherly speech
With one whose thought I had not hoped to reach.

"Men work together," I told him from the heart,
"Whether they work together or apart."

Three sonnets, three turns—in to the heart, out to the flowers (thanks to the butterfly), back to the heart and—from the heart—to the world. A solitary task one cannot do alone.

Frost, like many composers of music, lays down a theme he has picked up by turning to the world with his ears open. And like many composers of music, he attends to what he can see with his ears as well as what he can hear with his eyes. That is critical to the particular music of poetry, which (leaving the hearer aside for a moment) is for the reader as well as the writer a *visual* art that is an art of sound.

"Theme" is a musical term, and—though Frost is adamant that meaning is critical to poetry—it directs our attention to the melody more than the meaning of "The Tuft of Flowers" when we seek what it is he picks up from that poem in "Mending Wall."

"Mending Wall" is forty-five blank verse lines with no stanza breaks. One effect of this form is to slow the music down (though the meter doesn't change). The first fourteen lines can again be read as a sonnet ending with a couplet marked by the slant rhyme of "line" and "again." The turn comes in line nine with the gaps, from the presence of the wall to its absence. Lines thirteen and fourteen, read as a couplet, provide a resolution by resetting the wall:

Something there is that doesn't love a wall,
That sends the frozen-ground-swell under it,
And spills the upper boulders in the sun;
And makes gaps even two can pass abreast.
The work of hunters is another thing:
I have come after them and made repair
Where they have left not one stone on stone,
But they would have the rabbit out of hiding,
To please the yelping dogs. The gaps I mean,
No one has seen them made or heard them made,
But at spring mending-time we find them there.
I let my neighbour know beyond the hill;
And on a day we meet to walk the line
And set the wall between us once again.

But the next thirty-one lines turn the wall itself into a question, making the mending an outdoor game (in line twenty-one). The tone is light when the work is shown to be a game, with the neighbors walking a line and keeping the fence between them like the net in tennis. Each fields the stones that fall on his side—and speaks to them, using a spell to make them balance. The work is a game because there is no need for a wall, and the game is the making of the wall. The stones fall into place in the play between them. It is tempting to say that this is what playing tennis without a net might look like.

The tone turns serious (in line twenty-seven) when the neighbor quotes what the poet calls (in line forty-three) "his father's saying":

He only says, "Good fences make good neighbours."

It is interesting that this turn toward a more serious tone is one of only three places in the poem where Frost allows his strict pentameter to slip in an extra syllable. And it is interesting that the turn is marked by the I of the poem saying

Spring is the mischief in me, and I wonder
If I could put a notion in his head:

Recalling that spring is mending time, it seems to me that Frost is making hay of metaphor again by putting it to work in sorting through what the saying of the father(s) is walling in and walling out:

"Why do they make good neighbors? Isn't it
Where there are cows? But here there are no cows.
Before I built a wall I'd ask to know
What I was walling in or walling out,
And to whom I was like to give offence.

(Clearly, the mischief includes puns that might evoke a groan as well as a smile...)

Something there is that doesn't love a wall,
That wants it down." I could say "Elves" to him,
But it's not elves exactly, and I'd rather
He said it for himself. I see him there
Bringing a stone grasped firmly by the top
In each hand, like an old-stone savage armed.
He moves in darkness as it seems to me,
Not of woods only and the shade of trees.
He will not go behind his father's saying,
And he likes having thought of it so well
He says again, "Good fences make good neighbors."

The poem does what it describes—at least in the play between participants in the dialogue: it mends a wall that is not necessary.

I read every one of the fifteen narrative poems in *North of Boston* as a variation on the wall. Consider "The Mountain," which begins with these eighteen lines:

> The mountain held the town as in a shadow
> I saw so much before I slept there once:
> I noticed that I missed stars in the west,
> Where its black body cut into the sky.
> Near me it seemed: I felt it like a wall
> Behind which I was sheltered from a wind.
> And yet between the town and it I found,
> When I walked forth at dawn to see new things,
> Were fields, a river, and beyond, more fields.
> The river at the time was fallen away,
> And made a widespread brawl on cobble-stones;
> But the signs showed what it had done in spring;
> Good grass-land gullied out, and in the grass
> Ridges of sand, and driftwood stripped of bark.
> I crossed the river and swung round the mountain.
> And there I met a man who moved so slow
> With white-faced oxen in a heavy cart,
> It seemed no harm to stop him altogether.

Not a sonnet, quite; but quite like one—and it repeats the theme before it turns on an encounter that stops *both* altogether. What happens after the turn is another kind of outdoor game. There is no net, and yet they volley:

> Where is your village? Very far from here?
> There is no village—only scattered farms...
> That looks like a path. Is that the way to reach the top from here?

There is no proper path...
You've never climbed it?
I've been on the sides...

There is a brook at the mountain's summit that is "cold in summer, warm in winter."

That ought to be worth seeing.
If it's there. You never saw it?
I guess there's no doubt about its being there. I never saw it.

And in the play, a series of contrasts:

...a good distance down might not be noticed
By anyone who'd come a long way up.

It doesn't seem so much to climb a mountain
You've worked around the foot of all your life.

...leading back to the first contrast and an observation that is a comment on the whole:

"Warm in December, cold in June, you say?"

"I don't suppose the water's changed at all.
You and I know enough to know it's warm
Compared with cold, and cold compared with warm.
But all the fun's in how you say a thing."

In the play of words lies the fun of how you say, and how you say plays a critical role in contrasts that we feel like a wall as sure as a mountain.

"A Servant to Servants" is a dramatic monologue that sheds new light on playing tennis without a net. Not only is there no net in this poem, there is no partner. But putting it that way risks missing the point. A net we do not see is not no net, and a partner out of sight who we do not hear is not nobody. Let's not forget that the poet is making hay. And this poem walks the line keeping the wall between the players even more dramatically than "Mending Wall."

The poem, not broken into stanzas, begins in the middle (don't they all?) with what, again, not quite a sonnet, looks and sounds quite like a sonnet:

> I didn't make you know how glad I was
> To have you come and camp here on our land.
> I promised myself to get down some day
> And see the way you lived, but I don't know!
> With a houseful of hungry men to feed
> I guess you'd find....It seems to me
> I can't express my feelings any more
> Than I can raise my voice or want to lift
> My hand (oh, I can lift it when I have to).
> Did ever you feel so? I hope you never.
> It's got so I don't even know for sure
> Whether I am glad, sorry, or anything.
> There's nothing but a voice-like left inside
> That seems to tell me how I ought to feel,
> And would feel if I wasn't all gone wrong.

What happens in the sixth line of that sequence (*I guess you'd find....It seems to me*) is interesting musically—eight syllables, ten beats. The ellipsis and period (visually, four dots) could be indicated by two rests, an instance of a poem acting like a score when we perform it as readers.

"All gone wrong," a woman who struggles with madness—the I of the poem—recalls the madness of her father's brother, who had been, literally, caged rather than being sent to an asylum. That caging comes to mind in her account of her own life—the real presence of a memory in what she says of a life she is in the middle of living now. *You take the lake*, it begins, *I look and look at it.*

> *I see it's a fair, pretty sheet of water.*
> *I stand and make myself repeat out loud*
> *The advantages it has, so long and narrow,*
> *Like a deep piece of some old running river*
> *Cut short off at both ends. It lies five miles*
> *Straight away from the mountain notch*
> *From the sink window where I wash the plates,*
> *And all our storms come up toward the house,*
> *Drawing the slow waves whiter and whiter.*
> *It took my mind off doughnuts and soda biscuit*
> *To step outdoors and take the water dazzle*
> *A sunny morning, or take the rising wind*
> *About my face and body and through my wrapper,*
> *When a storm threatened from the Dragon's Den,*
> *And a cold chill shivered across the lake.*

The thought of the lake—and the storms off the lake—suffices to turn her, and she asks her silent partner how he came to hear of Willoughby. We hear his answer in her repetition—a declarative contained—as so often happens—in an interrogative: *In a book about ferns? Listen to that!* (And here another note to Adorno:

Language, like music, often makes us hear what is not there in what is, the stutter step between a sound we do not hear and the echo we do. Here, our eyes are directed to something spoken off the page.)

Listen to that! points both ways—back to what is echoed in the interrogative and forward to what follows:

You let things more like feathers regulate
Your going and coming. And you like it here?

(We know, of course, that hope is the thing with feathers...)

I can see how you might. But I don't know!
It would be different if more people came,
For then there would be business. As it is,
The cottages Len built, sometimes we rent them,
Sometimes we don't. We've a good piece of shore
That ought to be worth something, and may yet.
But I don't count on it as much as Len.
He looks on the bright side of everything,
Including me. He thinks I'll be all right
With doctoring. But it's not medicine—
Lowe is the only doctor's dared to say so—
It's rest I want—there, I have said it out—
From cooking meals for hungry hired men
And washing dishes after them—from doing
Things over and over that just won't stay done.
By good rights I ought not to have so much
Put on me, but there seems no other way.
Len says one steady pull more ought to do it.
He says the best way out is always through.
And I agree to that, or insofar
As that I can see no way out but through—
Leastways for me—and then they'll be convinced.

Standing at the sink window, storms off the lake take her mind off doing / *Things over and over that just won't stay done.* Her husband, looking "on the bright side," thinks medicine will make her "all right." He speaks of the "best" way, which she says she accepts because she sees no other way.

And that leaves her (and us) with an extravagance of grief, not thinking about making the world better but thinking about making it work.

And, again, making it work is a sort of game in which the players keep the wall between them:

> We have four here to board, great good-for-nothings,
> Sprawling about the kitchen with their talk
> While I fry their bacon. Much they care!
> No more put out in what they do or say
> Than if I wasn't in the room at all.
> Coming and going all the time, they are:
> I don't learn what their names are, let alone
> Their characters, or whether they are safe
> To have inside the house with doors unlocked.
> I'm not afraid of them, though, if they're not
> Afraid of me. There's two can play at that.

What makes her think they have as much reason to be afraid of her as she of them is that not only is she not "all right" but not being at all "right" runs in the family:

> My father's brother wasn't right. They kept him
> Locked up for years back there at the old farm.
> I've been away once—yes, I've been away.
> The State Asylum. I was prejudiced;
> I wouldn't have sent anyone of mine there;
> You know the old idea—the only asylum
> Was the poorhouse, and those who could afford,
> Rather than send their folks to such a place,
> Kept them at home; and it does seem more human.

In the making and mending of walls, it seems to me, Frost inquires after facts. And the facts he lights on are invariably moments in the process of an act. Home seems more human, but it's not. And, again, that evokes grief more than grievance, as in the detailed description of what it meant for the uncle of the I of this poem to be at home:

> *Cruel—it sounds. I 'spose they did the best*
> *They knew. And just when he was at the height,*
> *Father and mother married, and mother came,*
> *A bride, to help take care of such a creature,*
> *And accommodate her young life to his.*
> *That was what marrying father meant to her.*

She knew the uncle, who was before her time, by stories the family told—

> *But the pen stayed exactly as it was*
> *There in the upper chamber in the ell,*
> *A sort of catch-all full of attic clutter.*

And she, half-joking, would say

> *"It's time I took my turn upstairs in jail"—*
> *Just as you will till it becomes a habit.*

And now she says

> *I 'spose I've got to go the road I'm going:*
> *Other folks have to, and why shouldn't I?*
> *I almost think if I could do like you,*
> *Drop everything and live out on the ground—*

"I've got to go the road I'm going" looks like a statement of fact, but it is a question like "*Why* do they make good neighbors?" Walking the line, keeping the wall between them, between, as at the end of this poem, "I'd rather and you must."

I turn, finally, to "Christmas Trees," from Frost's third collection, *Mountain Interval*, published in 1916, which combines elements, both lyric and narrative, of his first two collections, *A Boy's Will* and *North of Boston*. This third collection is an extended meditation on space and time (keeping in mind that an interval may be a matter of either or both, particularly where and when it is a matter of mountains) after the meditation on boundaries and boundary crossing that formed *North of Boston*. "The Road Not Taken" introduces the theme brilliantly as it combines lyric with narrative: we are in the present of the speaker of the poem, but in that present we share an imagined time "somewhere ages and ages hence." Imagining that time in the poet's present, we may forget that we are reading the poem—perhaps reading it with a sigh—in one of those "ages and ages hence," our own age, a *where* as much as a *when* in the language of the poem.

In "Christmas Trees," the *where* and the *when* get teased out where city meets country—an intersection understood as a boundary where beings meet other beings (human and otherwise) in nature.

This boundary, like the wall in "Mending Wall," has gaps in it, and the two sides interpenetrate:

> *The city had withdrawn into itself*
> *And left at last the country to the country;*
> *When between whirls of snow not come to lie*
> *And whirls of foliage not yet laid, there drove*
> *A stranger to our yard, who looked the city,*
> *Yet did in country fashion in that there*
> *He sat and waited till he drew us out*
> *A-buttoning coats to ask him who he was.*

"Looking the city," it seems, implies an expectation of impatience. "Country fashion," on the other hand, implies waiting with the intention of drawing the other out—patience, not passivity. One who "looks the city" but waits to draw the other out blurs the lines. Beings meeting other beings constitute boundaries where movement takes place—advancing and withdrawing, giving form to both city and country, each an other to the other. It is interesting in this regard that Frost wrote (in commenting on Amy Lowell's poetry) that "the most exciting movement in nature is expansion and contraction."

The stranger proves to be *the city come again / to look for something it had left behind...*

Something left behind suggests either something one had but has lost or something one had intended to take but didn't. Either way, there is an assumption of ownership—and the poem, it seems, takes that assumption to be characteristic of the city. This is attached to Christmas by way of coming and coming again, a trope familiar from the literature(s) of Christianity. The city has come *here* to look for something it does not have *there*, something it *must* have to keep its Christmas. "Its Christmas" suggests a Christmas that might be different from the country's Christmas, and that precipitates a turn:

> He asked if I would sell my Christmas trees;
> My woods—the young fir balsams like a place
> Where houses all are churches and have spires.
> I hadn't thought of them as Christmas trees.

Thinking of them as Christmas trees rather than as woods turns the I of the poem to *the trial by market everything must come to.* Must. Are we now about mending another wall that is not necessary?

What follows plays, it seems to me, with what each can and cannot see. The stranger can't see the forest for the trees, and the I of the poem can see nothing but. When the stranger counts the trees that will be cut, he says "a thousand"—and the I of the poem responds:

"A thousand Christmas trees—at what apiece?"

He felt some need of softening that to me:
"A thousand trees would come to thirty dollars."

Now the stranger speaks in terms of the whole—but only to soften the contrast between the extent of the woods that would be stripped bare and the value attached to every single tree.

I've been making hay in this talk of turning grass, mending walls, meeting friends and strangers keeping walls between them minding gaps, facing memories that bring the going out of what we call city, the drawing out of what we call country, the real city that happens nowhere but in between, to mind. Minding gaps and balancing stones with spells while we pause to consider to whom we might be giving a fence with words we weave to draw them out in worlds of words to the end is, I think, what poets do. The frozen-ground-swell of repeated frost that makes gaps in walls even two can pass abreast is something to celebrate (even when we moan this time of year about the roadwork that follows the gaps it also makes in pavement). And I think one of Frost's greatest gifts was his embrace of the mischief in him in poetry, an art he said was a kind of fooling—which means, by extension, that the poet is a kind of fool. And knowing something of the role fools play in the shaping of history (from our reading of Shakespeare if not from direct experience), that sheds some light on Shelley's unacknowledged legislators.

There are, Frost wrote, "many things I have found myself saying about poetry, but the chiefest of these is that it is metaphor, saying one thing and meaning another, saying one thing in terms of another, the pleasure of ulteriority. Poetry is simply made of metaphor. So also is philosophy—and science, too, for that matter, if it will take the soft impeachment from a friend..." The matter of language, the matter of poetry, is metaphor, and its pleasure is ulteriority.

And that—as we used to say of something we happened upon and found remarkable—is something else.

SEVEN
Unacknowledged Legislators

¶ Not long ago, a tweet appeared in my twitter timeline from a booklover who had just wandered into Powells for the first time. (Technically, it was a *retweet* that came my way because I "follow" Powells.) As it happens, this was in Oregon. But it could just as easily have been in Chicago—and when I tell the story again, I may move it here for home field advantage. (We all know this is, in any case, where every story of Powells ultimately begins.)

The original tweeter was all atwitter about having found a *really* old book. I'm a sucker for old books (as I suspect just about everybody in this room is), so I expanded the tweet to see the photo that came with it, the moment captured, as almost every moment now is, on a smartphone.)

I can't remember the title (I'll probably insert an appropriate one later when I move the story to Chicago—Wayne Booth's *Rhetoric of Irony* perhaps?) but the date sticks: 1974.

My teacher Dick Luecke used to tell us (quoting John of Salisbury) that we read ancient texts to improve our eyesight. It is illuminating to be reminded that some of the ancient texts that help us see more clearly were published in our lifetimes.

My focus today will be a text, Percy Shelley's "Defence of Poetry," that was written and published before our time. (It was written in 1821, in response to Thomas Love Peacock's 1820 "Four Ages of Poetry," and published posthumously in 1840.) But I read it with a more recent text (Ed Reed's *From Soul to Mind*) in mind. Writing in the mid-1990s, Reed encouraged us to turn to 19th century literature (rather than philosophy) for the roots of the modern science of psychology. I'll have to save an extended discussion of Reed's work for another time—but I think that taking the turn he suggested can help us see why mind is such a weighty matter in Shelley's "Defence."

¶ Peacock begins with an epigraph from the *Satyricon* of Petronius, which was probably written in the first century, when Nero was emperor: "People fed on this kind of thing have as much chance of becoming wise as those who inhabit the kitchen have of being fragrant." Latin was still the language of scholars who wanted to be sure people knew they were scholars when Peacock wrote, so it stands to reason that a satirist who wanted to coax us into a "scholarly" state of mind would turn to a fragment of a satire and quote it in Latin. That "this kind of thing" is unspecified in this fragment (though it is not unspecified in the *Satyricon*) lets us know up front that we are going to have to make a judgment about just what this kind of thing *is*. The most likely candidates would be poetry (about which the essay is written) or the essay itself (which, given what we know of the author, we expect to have something of satire in it). For our purposes, the most important question will be how Shelley decides this.

He follows with a simple statement that he will proceed to illuminate in the essay: "Poetry, like the world, may be said to have four ages, but in a different order: the first age of poetry being the age of iron; the second, of gold; the third, of silver; and the fourth, of brass." Peacock assumes his readers will recognize Ovid behind this (and Hesiod behind Ovid). His reordering means that the first age of poetry corresponds to the last age of the world.

That first age of poetry, its iron age, is one in which everyone is a warrior and "rude bards celebrate in rough numbers the exploits of ruder chiefs." The "practical maxim of every form of society, 'to keep what we have and catch what we can,'" has not yet been disguised as justice or law. "In these days," he writes, "the only three trades flourishing (besides that of priest which flourishes always) are those of king, thief, and beggar: the beggar being for the most part a king deject, and the thief a king expectant. The first question asked of a stranger is, whether he is a beggar or a thief: the stranger, in reply, usually assumes the first, and awaits a convenient opportunity to prove his claim to the second appellation." We can rest assured that in this first age of poetry the poet belongs to one of these categories, because there is nowhere else to go: the poet must be king, beggar, thief, or priest. Peacock sets the priest apart, so we are left, for now, with king, beggar, or thief. No one expects the poet to be king, so we are left with beggar or thief. And Peacock leads us to believe the beggar is only looking for an opportunity to be a thief— and everyone is out to be a king. So we are most likely to meet the poet the way we meet every stranger in this iron age, as a beggar waiting for the opportunity to become a thief and ascend the throne.

Peacock writes of "the natural desire of every man to engross to himself as much power and property as he can acquire by any means which might makes right" that is accompanied by "the no less natural desire of making known to as many people as possible the extent to which he has been a winner in this universal game." This is where the poet enters. "The successful warrior becomes a chief; the successful chief becomes a king; his next want is an organ to disseminate the fame of his achievements and the extent of his possessions; and this organ he finds in a bard, who is always ready to celebrate the strength of his arm, being first duly inspired by that of his liquor. This is the origin of poetry, which, like all other trades, takes its rise in the demand for the commodity, and flourishes in proportion to the extent of the market." It seems Peacock knows his Adam Smith as well as his Hobbes (perhaps, as a satirist, well enough to use them both as straight men).

The point—and this will prove important for our reading of Shelley—is that poetry is "panegyrical" in its origin.

As Peacock lays this out, poetry's "iron age" predates written language. The poetry of this age is "numerically modulated," devoted to the enumeration of the king's battles and possessions. The numerical modulation, he says "is at once useful as a help to memory, and pleasant to the ears of uncultured men, who are easily caught by sound." Peacock notes that, as is typical of any undertaking, some people are exceptionally good at this counting and recounting—and they are celebrated, like Demodocus in the *Odyssey* and Thamyris in the *Iliad*. What sets them apart is that "they are observing and thinking, while others are robbing and fighting: and though their object be nothing more than to secure a share of the spoil, yet they accomplish this end by intellectual, not by physical, power: their success excites emulation to the attainment of intellectual eminence: thus they sharpen their own wits and awaken those of others, at the same time that they gratify vanity and amuse curiosity."

The second, golden, age of poetry "finds its materials in the age of iron." It begins "when poetry begins to be retrospective." Peacock sees the first age of poetry as one in which poets have a virtual monopoly on intellectual activity and on the audience interested in such activity. In the second age, though, as social institutions emerge, people begin to "live more in the light of truth and within the interchange of observation." They notice that—if they are to believe the tales the poets tell—they don't encounter gods with the same frequency as their ancestors, and they reach two conclusions: that the age is degenerate and that they are less in favor with the gods than were their ancestors. In the age of iron, poets learn to surround rulers and ruling families with traditions that invest them with power, magnificence, and proximity to the gods. They reach a point at which nothing they can say about a current ruler is sufficiently magnificent to avoid "being kicked for flimsy flattery" as Peacock says. So they learn to praise current leaders by praising them through their ancestors. The perfection of this art of praise is the age of Homer, the golden age of poetry. "Poetry has now attained its perfection: it has attained the point which it cannot pass: genius therefore seeks new forms for the treatment of the same subjects." New fields of literature, notably history, arise: "the maturity of poetry may be considered the infancy of history." Peacock suggests that "speculations... and disputes on the nature of man and of mind; on moral duties and on good and evil; on the animate and inanimate components of the visible world... begin to draw off from poetry a portion of its once undivided audience."

This leads to the third, silver, age, which Peacock calls "the poetry of civilized life." It is of two kinds—"imitative and original." Imitative poetry recasts the poetry of the golden age (he cites Virgil as the obvious example). Original poetry, he says, is "comic, didactic, or satyric" (Menander, Aristophanes, Horace, Juvenal). "Civilized" poetry "is characterized by an exquisite and fastidious selection of words, and a laboured and somewhat monotonous harmony of expression: but its monotony consists in this, that experience having exhausted all the varieties of modulation, the civilized poetry selects the most beautiful, and prefers the repetition of these to ranging through the variety of all. But the best expression being that into which the idea naturally falls, it requires the utmost labour and care so to reconcile the inflexibility of civilized language and the laboured polish of versification with the idea intended to be expressed, that sense may not appear to be sacrificed to sound. Hence numerous efforts and rare success." This exerts pressure against "ornamental and figurative language" in favor of "the simplest and most unvarnished phrase." Poetry can't keep up as reason gains ascendancy over imagination and feeling, so "the empire of thought is withdrawn from poetry, as the empire of facts had been before." Peacock summarizes: "the poet of the age of gold celebrates the heroes of the age of iron; the poet of the age of silver re-casts the poems of the age of gold." The range is limited, and the poetry finally becomes wearisome. Poetry "must either cease to be cultivated, or strike into a new path. Poetry turns to the multitudes yawning for amusement, and gaping for novelty."

This is the age of brass, which rejects the polish and learning of the age of silver, takes a "retrograde stride to the barbarisms and crude traditions of the age of iron," and "professes to return to nature and revive the age of gold." This, Peacock says, is "the second childhood of poetry," which replaces "the comprehensive energy of the Homeric Muse, which, by giving at once the grand outline of things, presented to the mind a vivid picture in one or two verses, inimitable alike in simplicity and magnificence with a verbose and minutely-detailed description of thoughts, passions, actions, persons, and things, in that loose rambling style of verse, which any one may write, *stans pede in uno* [standing on one foot], at the rate of two hundred lines in an hour."

Up to this point, Peacock has written as though he is engaged in a quasi historical account that works alongside Ovid's four ages read as history. The world begins with an idyllic and peaceful age of gold and gradually degenerates into a brutal state of permanent war in which everyone is a warrior. Poetry emerges in that age of iron. It inadvertently contributes to the civilization of the warrior society by creating a space for rational activity. That ultimately leaves poetry homeless, and it degenerates into something that is simply mindless.

Where I grew up, we'd say, for poets, "them's fightin' words."

That Peacock isn't simply or straightforwardly passing off what he's doing as a kind of history (and that he is yanking his friend Shelley's chain while, with Shelley, yanking the chain of the powers that be) is made clear when he recapitulates the four ages in modern poetry. "To the age of brass in the ancient world," he writes, "succeeded the dark ages, in which the light of the Gospel began to spread over Europe, and in which, by a mysterious and inscrutable dispensation, the darkness thickened with the progress of the light. The tribes that overran the Roman Empire brought back the days of barbarism, but with this difference, that there were many books in the world, many places in which they were preserved, and occasionally some one by whom they were read, who indeed (if he escaped being burned *pour l'amour de Dieu,*) generally lived an object of mysterious fear, with the reputation of magician, alchymist, and astrologer." As Europe emerged from this barbarism, the ancient age of iron was replicated, and poetry emerged, as it had before, in response to Market forces. Warriors everywhere meant a proliferation of chiefs that created a demand for bards to sing their praises. This new warrior society served as a "picturesque field" for "the two great constituents of poetry, love and battle."

Peacock repeats the cycle for modern poetry (with a decidedly Anglocentric spin). The age of Shakespeare, of course, is the golden age that follows the age of iron that accompanies the rise of Europe (and England as the Europe of Europe?). Milton, who Peacock identifies as the greatest poet of the English language, stands alone between the age of gold and the age of silver. And it's downhill from there, ending with the Lake poets, which, of course, includes Shelley.

If Peacock is indeed baiting his friends (as I think he is), he takes the predictable (but effective) tack of placing the circle that includes them (and, presumably, himself with them) at the point where poetry, having created a space for reason, loses its mind and becomes nothing but performance. Serious thought takes place elsewhere, and people of talent do something else.

II

¶Being a good friend, a good poet, and having a better sense of humor than he's usually given credit for, Shelley takes the bait. And he takes it the way the most successful guests on the Colbert Report or the Daily Show have taken it over the years—by keeping in mind that this is not an argument in the usual sense but an opportunity to make a scene.

The Colbert Report is probably the better analogue, because Peacock has taken on a role like that of a conservative talk show host and deployed the weapons of what we would now call neoliberal economics (it wasn't "neo" yet when he wrote) to airbrush poetry out of history as we make it now: the poet may have been but is not now a maker of history. And, in this context, a poet who simply insists on his or her importance will look a lot like a performer standing on one foot while spinning out verse at the rate of two hundred lines an hour. And the case is made for the character Peacock is playing.

What's a poet to do? Shelley turns his attention to the scene-making itself as the making of history, the scene in which politics takes shape. He sets out to offer, as he says in a letter to Peacock, an antidote—not a rebuttal to the essay, but a scene that takes it in.

One of the difficulties in reading this bit of Shelley is that we routinely encounter it in isolation and in defensive posture, with the most famous line ("poets are the unacknowledged legislators of the world") as the conclusion to an argument. We read it as a bit of Shelley, not as a bit Peacock and Shelley made between them the way Abbott and Costello made "Who's on first?" (I don't mean to say it's as funny as "Who's on first?" but it does have its moments—which we lose if we read Shelley's essay in isolation.)

The line in question falls in the middle, at the end of the first part of what was to be in three parts. The first part was written in 1821, intended for publication in the same magazine where Peacock's "Four Ages" had appeared. Both the magazine and Shelley died before any of the three parts were published—and the first part—which it seems was the only one written—was published (without the essay to which it responds) in 1840. Given that isolation, it is all too easy to forget that the posture is "defensive" in the way two friends sparring verbally are defensive—as if the poet Peacock had said to the poet Shelley, "Shelley, when are you going to get a real job?"

It seems to me that Shelley decides the question with which we began by ignoring both of the most likely candidates and taking the economic framework Peacock assumes and the four ages he describes as "the kind of thing" to which the epigraph is meant to refer. Among what kind of thing, he seems inclined to ask, *is* one likely to grow wise? And he answers the hypothetical question I just posed by getting down to work.

The two main points of contact for this bit are the meaning and scope of mental activity and where poetry begins.

What does mind do, where does it do it, and what does it have to do with poetry (or vice versa). Peacock plays the rational choice economist (or, better, the popularizer of rational choice economics) for whom the only use of poetry is as praise song for the hero and the only motivation to be a poet is to get as close to power as possible. He lets his character be thoughtful enough to allow for a civilizing spinoff when poetry creates a place for reason in the midst of endless war. But he abandons poetry as soon as that place is made: there is nothing to mind but reason and reason is nothing but self-interested choice. Once we have that, poetry loses its utility.

Shelley takes up the question of adult play (and Mary Shelley, as Reed notes, does this even more effectively than Percy) by asserting a play of mind beyond self-interested choice. Peacock says poetry begins in panegyric. Percy says it begins in song and dance and imitation of nature.

Some years ago, I heard an interview with David Steinberg, one of the great masters of improvisational theater, in which he said that one of the keys to improv was to take what is given to you by your collaborator(s) and *play* with it. If your collaborator walks on stage as a psychiatrist, play a patient undergoing analysis. And if your collaborator is a devotee of a popular version of rational choice economics who has just removed the ground on which the poet stands, play the poet standing. Making a scene is both placing and taking place—and in the improvisation we routinely do when we play with friends, the question is who places whom. The poet, Percy suggests, is not out of his or her mind; the mind is out of the poet—and, here and now, he adds, it is between you and me.

If your partner stays in character as a devotee of "rational choice." arguing against it will get you nowhere. But (if you have an audience) demonstrating a mind that can contain both reason and poetry at work may shed a little light.

Shelley begins with two classes of mental action, making a distinction between reason and imagination. But he associates each with a Greek term that turns it—reason (το λογιζειν) is analytic and passive, and imagination (το ποιειν), is synthetic and active. Reason is the mind "contemplating the relations borne by one thought to another." Imagination is the mind "acting upon those thoughts... composing from them... other thoughts." Reason contemplates relations rather than thoughts, and imagination acts on the thoughts themselves. Reason is primarily concerned with differences among things (so it focuses on making distinctions) while imagination is primarily concerned with similarities among things (so it focuses on discerning patterns). If reason talks, imagination walks—a bit like disproving Zeno's paradox by walking (from A to B).

Human beings, Shelley says, "dance and sing and imitate natural objects." The origin of dance and song is imitation, and human beings observe "a certain rhythm or order" in the act of imitation. It is the rhythm and order of the act of imitation (not the rhythm and order of the objects imitated) that catch Shelley's eye. In building his "defence" of poetry, Shelley focuses first on the observation of the act of imitation. Everyone, he says, observes a similar—but not an identical—order. Those similar orders are judged by the degree of their approximation to an order from which "the highest delight" results. Those in whom the "faculty of approximation to the beautiful... exists in excess," he says, "are poets, in the most universal sense of the word. Shelley's attention is on the manner in which they express the influence of society or nature upon their own minds." So the faculty is important, but the expression of the effect that faculty apprehends is critical. According to Shelley, it consists in language that is "vitally metaphorical"—alive with metaphor, marking relations of things that were previously unapprehended. It makes relations visible that were not visible before—and, in time, it makes the words that represent these relations "signs for portions and classes of thoughts, instead of pictures of integral thoughts." Through the poet's imaginative act, we see relations we could not see before. Those relations gradually lose their integrity and require the vitally metaphorical language of new poets to create new associations that make the language live again. Shelley cites Bacon's observation that these relations are "the same footsteps of nature impressed upon the various subjects of the world." The faculty that apprehends them is "the storehouse of axioms common to all knowledge," and the person most in possession of that faculty is the poet. In the beginning, everyone is necessarily a poet, because language is poetry. To be a poet is "to apprehend the true and the beautiful, in a word the good which exists in the relation, subsisting, first between existence and perception, and secondly between perception and expression."

Shelley constructs a series of relations, each of which builds upon the others: in the expression of the perception of existence, he attends to relations between the expression and the perception, between the perception and the existence—and, within existence, between imitation and the objects imitated. Poetry is prior to philosophy and science not in the sense of being less mature but in the sense of being more fundamental.

Shelley moves from a theory of mind to a theory of time when he speaks of the poet as both "legislator" and "prophet": "he not only beholds intensely the present as it is, and discovers those laws according to which present things ought to be ordered, but he beholds the future in the present, and his thoughts are the forms of the flower and the fruit of latest time." His point is not that poets can foretell the future but rather that "a poet participates in the eternal... [A]s far as relates to his conceptions time and place and number are not." The eternal is in time, and poetry is particularly attuned to it.

Speaking of poetry in a general sense, Shelley says that "language, colour, form, and religious and civil habits of action are all the instruments and materials of poetry; they may be called poetry by that figure of speech which considers the effects as a synonime of the cause." In a more restricted sense, poetry "expresses those arrangements of language, and especially metrical language which are created by that imperial faculty whose throne is curtained within the invisible nature of man." This, he says, "springs from the nature itself of language which is a more direct representation of the actions and the passions of our internal being, and is susceptible of more various and delicate combinations than colour, form or motion, and is more plastic and obedient to the control of that faculty of which it is the creation." Language is the clearest reflection of mind, poetry the purest form of language. The clearest view of mind is afforded by the use of language in poetry.

At this point, Shelley says we have circumscribed poetry within the art of which it is "the most perfect expression of the faculty itself." But to narrow the circle further, we must "determine the distinction between measured and unmeasured language; for the popular division into prose and verse, is inadmissible in accurate philosophy."

Both sounds and thoughts have relations "between each other and towards that which they represent, and a perception of the order of those relations, has always been found connected with a perception of the order of the relations of thoughts. Hence the language of poets has ever affected a certain uniform and harmonious recurrence of sound without which it were not poetry, and which is scarcely less indispensable to the communication of its influence, than the words themselves without reference to that peculiar order." It is this relation of sounds with each other, with thoughts, and with what they represent, that makes for "the vanity of translation." Sense—meaning—is not the obstacle to translation, but sound.

"A poem," Shelley writes, "is the very image of life expressed in its eternal truth." This wholeness is what sets the poem apart from the story. The story is "a catalogue of detached facts, which have no other bond of connexion than time, place, circumstance, cause and effect. The poem, on the other hand, attends to the unchangeable forms of human nature, as existing in the mind of the creator, which is itself the image of all other minds." This is not so much a dismissal of narrative as a claim about time in relation to thought: "a story of particular facts is as a mirror which obscures and distorts that which should be beautiful: Poetry is a mirror which makes beautiful that which is distorted."

Shelley shifts here from what poetry is (and who is a poet) to what poetry does—"its effects upon society."

The first effect is pleasure, which he traces to its acting "in a divine and unapprehended manner, beyond and above consciousness." Speaking of Homer's morally imperfect characters, Shelley says that "every epoch under names more or less specious has deified its particular errors... but a poet considers the vices of his contemporaries as the temporary dress in which his creations must be arrayed, and which cover without concealing the eternal proportions of their beauty."

Having turned from the aesthetic to the ethical, Shelley says that "the whole objection...of the immorality of poetry rests upon a misconception of the manner in which

poetry acts to produce the moral improvement of man."
While ethics is concerned with doctrines and examples of
"civil and domestic life," poetry "acts in another and a di-
viner manner. It awakens and enlarges the mind itself by
rendering it the receptacle of a thousand unapprehended
combinations of thought." Poetry makes the familiar unfamiliar, prompting its readers to think again. According
to Shelley, "the great secret of morals is Love; or a going
out of our own nature, and an identification of ourselves
with the beautiful which exists in thought, action or person, not our own. A man to be greatly good, must imagine intensely and comprehensively; he must put himself
in the place of another and of many others; the pains and
pleasures of his species must become his own. The great
instrument of moral good is the imagination: and poetry
administers to the effect by acting upon the cause. Poetry enlarges the circumference of the imagination by re-
plenishing it with thoughts of ever new delight... Poetry
strengthens the faculty which is the organ of the moral
nature of man in the same manner as exercise strengthens
a limb."

The "poetical faculty" has two functions: "it creates new
materials of knowledge, and power, and pleasure" and "it
engenders in the mind a desire to reproduce and arrange
them according to a certain rhythm and order, which may
be called the beautiful and the good."

Poetry "is the centre and circumference of knowledge."
This is a claim for mind's synthetic activity and so covers
an area broader than what we typically mean by "poetry."
"Poetry," he says, "is not like reasoning, a power to be exerted according to the determination of the will." Here,
Shelley distinguishes between the synthetic activity of
mind and the writing of the poem: "when composition
begins inspiration is already on the decline, and the most

glorious poetry that has ever been communicated to the world is probably a feeble shadow of the original conceptions of the poet." Shelley is convinced that "the greatest passages of poetry are not produced by labour and study." The question here is how labor and study are related to the conception of the whole—at both ends, in the poet and in the reader/hearer. Shelley develops an argument that has a great deal in common with Kandinsky. The point is not how to represent what was perceived but how to provoke the perception.

Shelley sees poetry as "the record of the happiest and best moments of the happiest and best minds," and that leads him to claim that "poetry thus makes immortal all that is best and most beautiful in the world..." In time, it stands against the ravages of time. It "redeems from decay the visitations of the divinity in man."

Returning to the synthetic function, Shelley asserts that poetry "subdues to union under its light yoke all irreconcilable things." In doing this, "it strips the veil of familiarity from the world, and lays bare the naked and sleeping beauty which is the spirit of its forms." Mind's synthetic activity drives toward unity in the practice of poetry, and that drive makes the familiar unfamiliar, provoking further synthetic activity.

Shelley's twist on "idealism" is that while "all things exist as they are perceived; at least in relation to the percipient... poetry defeats the curse which binds us to be subjected to the accident of surrounding impressions." Mind's synthetic activity enables the perception of wholes in a universe of fragmented experience: "it makes us the inhabitants of a world to which the familiar world is a chaos."

Shelley claims that "the greatest Poets have been men of the most spotless virtue," a claim that is certain to raise eyebrows among many readers familiar with his life. But he anticipates this in his description of Time as "mediator and redeemer." His point is that the errors of great poets weighed against the magnitude of their work are "dust in the balance." He adds to this the observation that "imputations of real and of fictitious crime have been confused in the contemporary calumnies against poetry and poets; consider how little is as it appears—or appears as it is; look to your own motives, and judge not, lest ye be judged." In short, look at the work, and recall how poetry's moral function works—not by the poet's being a role model but by strengthening imagination, "the faculty which is the organ of the moral nature of man."

Shelley repeats his distinction between synthetic and analytic activities of the mind, which he now refers to as "poetry" and "logic"—and he reiterates that poetry, unlike logic, "is not subject to the control of the active powers of the mind, and that its birth and recurrence has no necessary connexion with consciousness or will." The practice of poetry may cultivate a habit of seeing things whole— "an habit of order and harmony correlative with its own nature and with its effects upon other minds"; but in the intervals between inspiration, the poet sees the world the way everybody typically sees it, in pieces. Shelley essentially says that the poet's greater "sensitivity" is likely to make him or her more obnoxious in response to the chaos of everyday life. But this error is not "necessarily evil," and "the passions purely evil, have never formed any portion of the popular imputations on the lives of poets."

Summarizing, Shelley writes, "what is called poetry in a restricted sense has a common source with all other forms of order and of beauty according to which the materials of human life are susceptible of being arranged; and which is Poetry in an universal sense."

The second part, which was to have been "an application of these principles [described in part one] to the present state of the cultivation of Poetry," remains a promise that contains a lyrical description of the poet and culminates in the best known line of the essay: "Poets are the hierophants of an unapprehended inspiration, the mirrors of the gigantic shadows which futurity casts upon the present, the words which express what they understand not, the trumpets which sing to battle and feel not what they inspire: the influence which is moved not, but moves. Poets are the unacknowledged legislators of the World."

III

¶Most of Shelley's essay is a promise unfulfilled—but, between the realization of the first part and the promise of the rest, he raises a number of issues that are of critical importance not only for poetry but also for the still raging argument about the rule of law. Shelley's extended family included two acknowledged contributors to the way that argument took shape in the late eighteenth and early nineteenth centuries—William Godwin and Mary Wollstonecraft, the first a leading theorist of anarchism and the second a leading theorist of human rights. Anarchism comes in many flavors, but one feature that is common to all flavors is a deeply rooted suspicion of law itself (and hence the very idea of a "rule" of law). Theories of human rights, too, come in all shapes and sizes—and the variety has increased exponentially since the late eighteenth century. But a common theme of those that argue that there *are* human rights is the assumption that these "rights" can and should be formalized (often in declarations with the force of law). The issues Shelley raises in defense of poetry speak to both. I will state them here as theses, bearing in mind that the purpose of a thesis is to invite an argument.

First, law is not *imposed* by will but *discovered* by attention and imagination.

Second, the attention and imagination necessary for this discovery is rooted in a mathematical/musical distinction between measured and unmeasured language.

Third, the capacity to make that distinction is a cognitive activity with a lyric rather than a narrative structure.

The first of the three theses is broadly consistent with the Enlightenment confidence in the human capacity to know "right," but it puts Peacock's rational choice economist in his place. Shelley's distinction between poetry and (discursive) logic as activities of the mind broadens the concept of reason to include both—and (as Reed argues in his revision of the history of psychology) it puts mind in a place other than an individual's head. (Remember Marx's comment about Hegel—that he found him standing on his head and put him on his feet.) Follow Percy Shelley back to Mary Wollstonecraft then forward to Mary Shelley's *Frankenstein* and we find the rights of woman—and man—vindicated not in declarations made by national or international assemblies but in the acts of friends and strangers and the ways we embrace what we—and others—have made. God knows (and so do poets if we're paying attention) that making inanimate matter animate is no problem. The problem is turning living beings into objects that matter only to the extent that they are under control. Shelley, it seems to me, is putting some distance between power understood as control and the patterns that govern our lives as human beings in the world.

(I'd like to stop right here and break to read *Frankenstein*, the first eleven chapters of Genesis, and Coleridge's *Aids to Reflection*, then come back to have a serious discussion with the Shelleys, the Godwins, and the Wollstonecrafts about what it means to be like gods. But I don't suppose that's practical—at least in part because there would be no end to the texts we would be incited to read...)

So let's just say that creatures who are creators (and that means all of us) seem to have a hell of a time learning to love our creations (who are also creators) more than we fear them. And the prevalence of fear seems to make us think we are acting like gods when we think we have everything under control. This leads to the militarization of everything (Peacock's age of iron). And we have a pretty substantial dataset if we want to stop and consider how well that's worked out for us.

Note that this is perhaps the most important task Shelley assigns to poets: stopping to consider.

The second repudiates the popular distinction between poetry and prose and anticipates research in cognitive science that suggests a "musical" structure for the human brain (and/or its activity). The physical structure of the brain would likely be of less significance to Shelley than the structure of language and its relation to thought (or "mental activity"). But Shelley would have no difficulty embracing Marvin Minsky's assertion that mind is what brains do—which means that the two structures are intimately related. Our world may be a world of words to the end of it because our brains are constructed along musical lines. Language follows metrical patterns (in order of emergence), and measured language may be precisely the means by which we communicate patterns that govern our being in the world. Speaking of the definition of music as organized sound (which closely connects it with Shelley's measured language), Daniel Levitin notes that "the organization has to involve some element of the unexpected or it is emotionally flat and robotic." Emotionally flat, robotic, and *boring*, if we recall Charles Hartshorne's study of bird song. The critical element lies in a relationship—marked by what Hartshorne called the *threshold of monotony*. A creative work—whether its matter is sound and silence or pigment and paper—has to maintain a tension between giving us what we expect and giving us what we don't. This points—as does Shelley's insistence on imagination as *active*—not toward a simple matching of patterns "out there" with patterns "in here" but to a process of *constructing* patterns in which mind, brain, and world are actively engaged. Poem, as the *daxu* says, is where mind goes. And where would that be if not the world?

The third does not necessitate an either/or choice between lyric and narrative, but it may serve as a corrective to the large body of recent work in psychology that has understood the acting and perceiving self exclusively as *story*. Percy Shelley doesn't deny the temporal structure of human existence, and he certainly could spin a tale (though, as the famous contest that led to the composition of *Frankenstein* suggests, perhaps not quite as well as Mary). But his understanding of time gives the lyric glimpse of the whole in the parts a moral significance that is critical for the "unacknowledged" legislator. Putting some distance between law and the power to control does not deny that acknowledged legislators are most likely to be motivated by the *desire* to control and to depend on having the *power* to control. But, Shelley suggests (and I think there are echoes of Mary Wollstonecraft's understanding of rights here, especially the importance she places on education), the ability to perceive the patterns that enable human presence in the world is more fundamental than the desire or the power. (I am reminded of the brilliant depiction of the *hesitation* of Aeneas in Virgil's account of the founding of Rome, on which I believe the entire narrative turns. Without it, the poem is merely panegyric. With it, it may still be possible to dance.)

Talking about baseball in October is almost always more anticipation than presence for Chicagoans. It sets us to dreaming of spring at the first signs of winter. But, since I mentioned "Who's on first?" and made a disparaging comment about captured moments near the beginning of this talk, I want to end with an old baseball story that may not make sense much longer now that on field reviews have elevated moments captured on video to a status that allows second-guessing umpires to change the course of a game. For now, though, I think this still illustrates what it means to be a maker of law.

Three home plate umpires are talking about calling balls and strikes. The first says "I call 'em as I see 'em." The second says "I call 'em as they is." The third says "They ain't nothin' till I call 'em."

Enough said.

EIGHT
What Light Does On Edge

I

❡When I seek profound wisdom and penetrating insight into the nature of things, I almost always turn to cats or to sparrows. The persistence with which cats move to the periphery (as when an old cat follows a wall for the invisibility of it) makes them reliably critical observers who often see connections others miss. And sparrows have evolved far beyond us in their revolutionary patience and their ability to embrace what Dietrich Bonhoeffer characterized in his prison writing as the view from below—an early variant of the epistemological privilege of the oppressed, a key concept in liberation theology.

But I have found over the years that dogs can, with all four feet on the ground, sometimes take a bird's eye view that gives them almost feline insight. So I begin today with a philosopher dog who illustrates two key points around which this talk will circulate. A YouTube video has made the rounds, so I'm going to proceed with the assumption that some of you have seen it and that the rest of you will be able to find it if you're so inclined. In the spirit of thorough scholarly citation, I'll include a link in the notes that accompany the written version.

Let me sketch the scene for you. A dog (identified as a golden retriever in the video, though I think it's a yellow lab) stands at the threshold between two rooms, one of which appears to be newly carpeted. Someone on the other side, off camera (though we do see a shadow at one point) coaxes the dog to cross. He toes the line, studies it, can't bring himself to cross. Then he disappears for a moment before reappearing, tail first, backing toward the line. He backs over it, turns, and bounds to the person whose voice was calling.

Now, the two points.

First, in no uncertain terms, a line is not a thing to be taken lightly.

And, second, when one encounters a line that must be crossed, the best way to cross it may be backwards.

As you are no doubt aware, one thing always leads to another—so both points imply more than meets the eye (and, as Karl Marx and Virginia Woolf both noted, what meets the nose is sometimes as important in determining what we see). Each enfolds a complex set of interrelated subpoints.

Before I go on, a couple of notes and source citations.

As I mentioned, our philosopher dog holds forth on YouTube, which is arguably the most extensive repository of video (and often audio) documentation of animal behavior in the world today. It is fitting, I think, that our access to his demonstration is via a recording by an unidentified observer—in the manner of the student notes out of which our canonical versions of Aristotle's books are made. (And the shadow on the wall is a fleeting reminder of Aristotle's teacher, whose teacher, given his suspicion of books, might have entertained some doubts about this kind of video documentation.)

Less apparent, perhaps, are two sources that may be direct influences (the philosopher, though clearly a dog as thoughtful as Woolf's Flush, has not provided a bibliography, so we can't be certain) or may be instances of parallel insights achieved independently. The first is Kierkegaard, who said that history is lived forward but understood backward. This is evident both in the initial approach to the line and in the strategy for crossing it. The second is Leibniz, who believed that it is sometimes best to step back in order to leap forward (*reculer pour mieux sauter*). After encountering and examining the line between this and that (and there is a hint of Mohist logic here), our philoso-

pher dog turns to step nose first into what we can only assume is familiar territory, then reappears to illustrate that
great leaps forward may be made in reverse.

(The veiled reference to Chairman Mao is probably
more eisegesis than exegesis—but I put it on the table because, if you will allow the mixed metaphor here, it doesn't
matter if it's a white cat or a black cat. If it catches the
mouse it is a good cat.)

Which requires another note: every time I repeat this
staple of Chinese pragmatism (central to Deng Xiaoping's
opening and reform), I wonder about the epistemological
privilege of the mouse.

But let's return to our philosopher dog toeing the line.

We assumed (or I did—and I assume you went with me)
that the initial retreat was into familiar territory. This is
indicative of the frequency with which lines that come to
our attention—the lines we *see*—mark a division between
territory we consider to be familiar and territory we consider to be unfamiliar. This occurs so frequently that it
typically goes without saying.

You've all read Euclid, so you know our philosopher
dog crossed infinite lines with every step—but only one
stopped her in her tracks. Something about *this* side made
it possible to walk without stopping to think. Something
about *that* side made it impossible to do otherwise.

Between this and that is the line in question.

Our reading of Euclid also reminds us that a line is an
intersection of planes. The line is infinite in one dimension (length) while the plane is infinite in two dimensions
(length and width). The dog is a three dimensional body
traversing a two dimensional space (shades of Edwin A.
Abbott). From where the dog stands, the line does not look
like an intersection between two planes that are not parallel. It looks like a boundary between two territories. The

territories are not, strictly speaking, planes, because they are bounded (with lines on every side).

If the dog is seeing the line as a collision of two bounded infinites, it is no wonder she stops to think. Wouldn't you? Perhaps she turned to consult Zeno. Or Douglas Hofstadter.

In any case, we find ourselves with our philosopher dog leaping forward in reverse, from one infinity to another, crossing more lines than we can know between this and that.

II

¶Paul Klee described drawing as taking a line for a walk. One might say the same of poetry, which can be understood in part as the making of lines in the breaking of prose. As readers and writers of poetry, I suspect that all of you have encountered poems that feel more like a pack of lines taking you for a ride. And it wouldn't surprise me if there are makers and viewers of visual art here today who have had the same experience drawing—perhaps even in the drawing of Klee.

It occurs to me that some of you—wondering when I will get around to Goethe, O'Keeffe, or color—may be ready to apply that metaphor to what I'm doing here. It wouldn't be the first time. But I'd say we've been backing into the confluence of those three subjects from the beginning.

Let's turn to each now, and I'll see if I can shed a little more light to draw you in.

III

¶I attended a very small high school in Oldham County, Texas that had a number of distinct advantages critical to my development as a poet and visual artist.

First, I could walk no more than half an hour and be completely alone. When Georgia O'Keeffe was living not many miles away (in Randall County), she described the experience in a letter to her friend Anita Pollitzer: *nothing but to walk into nowhere...* Anyone who has experienced high school—as a student, as a member of the staff, as a parent—will understand the importance of escape in the process of education schooling is designed to contain. But there is also the experience of vision O'Keeffe caught in her correspondence with Pollitzer when she wrote from Canyon, Texas, *you have never seen SKY...* The place afforded an opportunity to escape, but it also provided an opportunity for almost unobstructed vision—the opportunity to be alone and see nothing. My friend and colleague Larry D. Thomas, who grew up in another part of West Texas, has also caught a bit of this in a collection of new and selected poems titled *As If Light Actually Matters*. He speaks there of sky as sacred text, to be read deeply the way one reads a work of philosophy—and of wind as *prophecy*. And, beginning with the grammatical construction of the title, he approaches light as a subject, matter as a verb: matter is what light does. More on this in a moment.

Second, because the school was so small, there were no large classes—and advanced academic classes usually ranged from two to four people, including the teacher. This took the form of an academic analogue to O'Keeffe's nothing but to walk into nowhere experience of the plains. A few steps beyond the basic curriculum and one was alone with the text (broadly understood, the way Thomas understands West Texas sky).

Third, I was fortunate to have teachers who had a good sense of when to get out of the way, a skill that is often undervalued in preparation and assessment of teachers.

Alone with the text, I was often free to follow my nose like our philosopher dog. One of the lines I encountered as a result is particularly important to my understanding of light and color and to my reading of Goethe and O'Keeffe.

In one of those small classes—just me and a recent college graduate who had been hired as a coach but had enough hours in science to meet the requirements in force at the time for a physics teacher at the high school level, I read the canonical account of light and color vision that drew an uninterrupted line from Newton's optics to the Young-Helmholtz theory to explain color vision in terms of three types of receptors, each sensitive to a range of wavelengths corresponding to the wavelengths of three primary colors.

By the time I took physics in high school, I had been painting for a number of years, so this account of color vision as an interplay of three receptors, each corresponding to a primary color, brought the pallette to mind. Long before Young-Helmholtz, painters knew that the entire range of colors (Newton's red-orange-yellow-green-blue-indigo-violet) could be created by mixing three pigments in various combinations. For me, those three were cadmium red, cadmium yellow, and cobalt blue. (Yes, I was into heavy metal in my own way.) But other reds, yellows, and blues would work—and the physiological evidence (speculation, really, because the instruments with which to make the physiological measurements came later) associated with these receptors suggested what many painters already knew, that the yellow pigment might be shifted toward blue. (Another note: I would later have long conversations with my father, who was a fine photographer, about the relative merits of Kodak and Fuji film. He favored Kodak, which shifted toward the red end of the spectrum, while I favored Fuji, which shifted toward blue.)

But optics is a theory of light, not pigment. So the interesting question for me was what happened when the two came together. Reading about color vision in a physics textbook had me thinking about the play of light as it relates to play with pigment in the practice of visual art. Newton, as a physicist devising an optics, was focused on the behavior of light—and especially on its commensurability, on metrics by which it might be measured and compared with other things. Shifting that focus toward physiology meant—in the canonical version—attending to what changed in bodies (and particularly bodily organs implicated in vision) touched by light. (I choose the verb "touch" deliberately here, with an eye on theorists from Berkeley to Alva Noë who have argued that vision is touch-like.) In general, the idea seemed to be that we needed to get from light (out there) to vision (in here) if we were going to get a sense of color.

That struck me then (as it strikes me now) as rendering vision, especially color vision, altogether too passive and too disengaged. And it also appeared to make both color and light more orderly, more cut and dried, than they had ever been in my experience. Continuing with the text, there was the matter of those other receptors (rods, as opposed to cones) that came into play especially in the twilight when (as Marx said in criticizing Hegel) all cats are gray. Leaving aside the fact that every cat knows (even in twilight) that not all cats are gray, these receptors that appeared to (mostly) ignore color (or frequency) to focus on intensity suggested that what was going on in color vision was more than measuring and mixing light reflecting off various surfaces.

It was here that my physics text introduced a short, tantalizing note about alternative theories and briefly described a series of experiments by Edwin H. Land that suggested the eye could reconstruct the full range of colors in a scene with information conveyed by black and white transparencies taken through different filters and superimposed on a screen. Based on these experiments, Land had proposed what he called the retinex theory of color vision as an alternative to Young-Helmholtz.

My father had a black and white Polaroid Land camera that had always fascinated me. (It made "instant" photos that developed in a matter of seconds right before your eyes, which seemed pretty magical in the pre-digital photography age.) So the name Land rang a bell, and I went off in search of the company's address. I wrote a letter to Land telling him that I was interested in his retinex theory and asking if he could send more information. A couple of months later (this was in an age that was not only pre-digital photography but also pre-email), I received two offprints from him that laid out the theory and described the experiments in more detail.

Much of this is familiar territory now, almost half a century later—so I'll spare you most of the detail. But the long and short of it is that he made two black and white transparencies of the same scene through two different colored filters—in effect, making two color desaturated records, one of which shifted toward the "short" end of the spectrum vis-a-vis the other. He then projected these transparencies through two different colored filters, superimposing them on a screen. What appeared there was a full-color image of the original scene.

There is a substantial body of literature on the interpretation and significance of these experiments (which began, as discoveries often do, with an accident. Land was actually projecting three images through three filters. One of the projectors was turned off, and an assistant noted how odd it was that the full range of colors still appeared on the screen). I'll be happy to point those of you who are interested to that body of literature—but, for now, I will again spare you most of the details, confining my comments to what I take to be most relevant to what we're doing today. Land interpreted the two color projection experiment to mean that there is more to vision (especially color vision) than meets the eye. His name for the theory associated with the experiment was coined to draw attention to the joint action of the retina and the cerebral cortex in the process of color vision.

By the time I was studying physiological psychology in college, the consensus was that the optic nerve should be understood as an extension of the brain and that processing began at the retina. The perceiving organism is more actively engaged in color vision than passive receptors of reflected light might suggest. Land also took into account the remarkable ability of human vision—not just the eye but also the brain—to maintain color consistency across wide variation in light intensity and quality. Those of you who are photographers may be familiar with the retinex algorithm sometimes employed in color correction during post processing of digital photos. Based on Land's theory, this is intended to make the camera act more like the human eye in its processing of color. It's also worth noting that William James considered this question in his theory of consciousness, making the turn one would expect of a pragmatist philosopher toward active engagement of the organism with the rest of the world. James was a visual artist, and, for him, the turn was prompted by the observation that we could perceive the green of the grass outside our window without being driven to distraction by the infinite variation of light and shade. Every photographer knows that cameras handle that differently than human eyes do. (And it might be interesting to track developments in digital photography that integrate the camera more fully into the computer and move processing closer and closer to the lens in a process that parallels the retinex system Land proposed.)

Land made it abundantly clear that he did not claim to be the first to question Newton's optics along these lines. He pointed specifically to Boyle and (most significantly for us today) Goethe. I filed the Goethe reference away when I read Land in high school, but (as interesting references are prone to do) it resurfaced. Reading Norwood Russell Hanson's *Patterns of Discovery* in a class with Richard Luecke, I came across a quotation from Goethe's *Farbenlehre*: "if the eye did not possess something of the sun, the sun could never be seen by it." That caught my eye, and it led me to dig a little deeper into Goethe and his color theory.

I keep sparing you details, and I suppose a turn to Goethe marks an opportune place and time to acknowledge that this is where the devil is often said to be. Before I do it again, I want to encourage you to read Goethe's work on color yourselves, with special attention to his style of experimental inquiry. Philosophers have taken note of his method and his response to Newton (Wittgenstein left an unfinished work on Goethe's color theory on his desk when he died), and cognitive scientists interested in color vision have embraced it with increasing frequency over the past half century.

What I find most interesting is that Goethe does not set out to simply prove Newton wrong. He sets out to engage and enlarge an argument—one he believes Newton truncated in ways that obstruct our vision. He does not object to Newton's finding that white light passed through a prism under carefully controlled conditions is refracted in such a way as to appear as a range of colors reflected from a white surface. He does object to the interpretation of this behavior as evidence that color is somehow contained in white light. Goethe's intuition, which he is willing to subject to rigorous experimental investigation, is that color cannot be contained.

This question of containment draws us back to the philosopher dog who got us started today. For color to be contained, a line would need to be drawn around it, and such a line would not be a thing to be taken lightly. Newton divided what he saw reflected from the surface on which white light passed through a prism was projected into seven colors, corresponding to the seven intervals in a musical octave. Goethe alerts us to pay attention not only to the lines Newton sees (why seven?) but also to those he does not see and to those he sees but does not *notice*.

IV

¶One way to respond to "why seven?" is by citing the influence of Kabbalah on Newton. That would not be an explanation, but it could prove illuminating.

There is no doubt that the power of number is critical to Kabbalah and that this power has been translated into an elaborate numerology in which seven has a place. Nor is there any doubt that Newton was influenced (as were many natural philosophers in 17th and 18th century Europe) by Lurianic Kabbalah in its Christianized version. But there is a place for every number in Kabbalah, and the range of light Newton saw on the wall could be divided into any number of categories. The association is perhaps most illuminating for what it does with light, which is understood to have contracted (*tsimtsum*) to make space for matter. One could say that in this account light does nothing on edge but *edges*. That rings true when one looks with O'Keeffe at light coming on—edging onto—the plains.

Another way to respond is by noting (as I did earlier) the analogy with music, important to both Newton and Goethe. The seven divisions of the spectrum correspond to the seven intervals of the musical scale that Newton and Goethe both took as normative. Combining the intervals of light would be analogous to combining the seven intervals in musical composition and performance. Composed (as in a painting or a scene), color would be like music.

That connection is interesting for several reasons (including O'Keeffe's interest in synesthesia). The colors of the spectrum are like the intervals of a scale. What happens in color vision (and art, as Blake would remind us, is nothing if not vision) is like music. That brings to mind Adorno's dictum that music is like language but it is not language. What happens in color vision is like music, but it is not music.

On the other hand, perhaps this vision/music/language troika is exactly what O'Keeffe had in mind when she said she found she could say things with color she could not say with words. That statement, in any case, assigns the same function to color and word within the universe of discourse. Both are for saying, though one may be better for saying this than that.

Hold that thought. We'll return to it—but first I want to pick up a thread exposed when I said citing the influence of Kabbalah or the seven tone scale wouldn't explain Newton's division of the spectrum into seven colors.

Why not? What is it we are doing when we explain?

It seems to me that more often than not what we are doing is bringing two territories (topics?)—one we take to be more familiar, one we take to be less—into contact. And that puts us right back with our philosopher dog toeing the line. What we call explanation (it seems to me) is something like using familiar territory to propel us over

264

the line we see between it and what we take to be unfamiliar. Cross that line often enough and it will disappear—at which point you are likely to replace *I'm lost* with *I know this*.

Strictly speaking, we cannot say what words do, though we know, saying, they do. Nor can we say what color does. But every one of us has said something like *I see* (perhaps by saying nothing) when a scene has touched us.

V

¶I mentioned Wittgenstein's unfinished commentary on Goethe's *Farbenlehre*. That unfinished work, published in English as *Remarks on Colour*, includes a number of important insights into what Goethe was doing. You will recall that Wittgenstein ended his *Tractatus* with a statement about what to do with what one cannot say. It is an exquisite rhymed couplet that, though it appears simple and straightforward, plunges us right into the heart of the matter: "*wovon man nicht sprechen kann, darüber muss man schweigen*" ("whereof one cannot speak, thereof one must be silent").

Wittgenstein's friend Bertrand Russell poked fun at him for having so much to say about what cannot be said. But it's important to remember that making this kind of joke (as both Kafka and Jesus seem to have understood) is one of the most effective ways to draw attention to the importance of this saying about what cannot be said for saying. Knowing a language (as Ivan Illich said) is as much about knowing the silences as knowing the sounds—and fluency is marked (like music) by how one handles the silences.

And this may help us get a better sense of what O'Keeffe had in mind when she said she could say in colors what she could not say in words. Given that she believes she *can* say in colors and that she sometimes speaks (as artists sometimes do) of what she is trying to say in a painting or a drawing, it is reasonable to assume that this falls in the category of what O'Keeffe *nicht sprechen kann* and the silence of her paintings speaks volumes. One might say the same of music, though it is not (always) silent. Both expand the universe of human discourse. And they do it (as I think Russell knew as well as Wittgenstein) by taking into account what is not said. Two books, as Wittgenstein put it: the one I have written and the one containing what I have not.

And there is that word "contain" again, the one that troubled Goethe. Goethe's objection is not to the kind of containment poets and painters routinely use in the telling of tales and the making of scenes. It is to the implication that colors are things and that light is a container.

For Goethe, light is an acting subject. The body of light may be a container (as any body may be), but to understand a body *simply* as a container—as a container and nothing more—is to get it wrong. Color, on the other hand, is an act—specifically, Goethe says, an act of light. So when we see color, we sense light acting—and that sense involves making a scene by seeing a surface marked (as our philosopher dog saw) by a line that functions as a boundary. I think this is what Wittgenstein had in mind when he said "a physical theory cannot solve the problem that motivated Goethe." Whether it can solve the problem that motivated Newton (or the problem that motivates us) is another question.

It is tempting (and a number of interpreters have succumbed) to distinguish Goethe's theory from Newton's by saying that Goethe's is psychological and Newton's is physical. But I think that is misleading in important ways.

Wittgenstein says Goethe's theory is not a theory at all. "Nothing," he writes, can be predicated by means of it. It is, rather, a vague schematic outline, of the sort we find in James' psychology. There is no experimentum crucis for Goethe's theory of colour. A vague schematic outline (ein vages Dankschema)—not a theory but a way of thinking along the lines of pragmatism, meaning that thought is embodied in action.

For the sake of parallel structure, shall we say like pragmatism but not pragmatism?

VI

¶Of course nothing is precisely what we must predicate to be silent.

I suggest that we approach this as we approached Adorno's comment on music. He said it is like language but not language, but we have taken the comment to enlarge the universe of human discourse and revise what we do when we say, what we mean when we say *language*.

In the same way, with reference especially to O'Keeffe, I suggest that we enlarge and revise our concept of pragmatism, which is inextricably connected with the *fact* as a moment in the *act*—not caught in the act but *perching* as James said.

Confronted not only with the plains but also with Palo Duro Canyon (the second largest in the United States), O'Keeffe described the problem of painting it as how to paint slits in nothing—nothing but to walk a line into nowhere while learning to see what one cannot say: *schweigen*.

That leads me, by way of conclusion, to this schematic of perceptual experience, drawing on Don Ihde's phenomenology of sound and those theorists who describe vision as touchlike—from Berkeley to Noë—that I referenced earlier:

Every perceptual experience is fundamentally tactile: it takes place when one body comes into contact with another. Touch, which has a spherical structure, is fundamental. It is localized in taste, which is directional (linear?).It is less obviously localized in vision, which is also directional. The experience of these two senses (taste and vision) is one of coming face to face. It takes wing in hearing and smell, both of which share its spherical structure. The experience of these two senses (hearing, and smell) is one of immersion. The experience of touch, localized and in flight, is face to face, immersed.

Face to face, immersed, the perfect painting is the perfect poem: silence, nothing more. Saying with color what one cannot say with words, one invites and makes way for silence—and that we cannot say except in passing.

Talking the talk is not walking
the walk. Naming a name means another
name. Name nothing, and the world begins.
Naming is the mother of ten thousand things.

Desire nothing, see wonder.
Desire more, see nothing
but what you happen

to see. One source, two names.
Say wonder, say wonder, say
wonder again. Open a door
on wonder upon wonder.

head and heart

Two things my mother told me
the day before she turned eighty four—

she woke up on her seventy second birthday
with "A Land Where We'll Never Grow Old"
in her head and five years ago when we
thought she was going to die she
heard a song she did not know
playing again and again.

She could not call it to mind, but
I asked her to hum it if it comes back
to her and send me a recording
so I could write it down.

It will, but she won't, because
she does not talk to machines.

Her heart doctor asked her if she remembered
when she was bleeding in the hospital and
she said no. She said she remembered
going in and she remembered
waking up: she asked
what that music was we'd been playing.

He thought she'd forgotten, but she told me
she wasn't there. She was in that song,
and a doctor of the heart (of all
people) should understand
that. He asked about bleeding
because he was changing her medication,
but he had memory in mind, counting backward

from a hundred by threes or some such thing.

One would think where the heart was would matter
most for one who cares for them and what song
is in it when. She says she always has a song
in her head and had always wanted
to work in a flower shop and make hats.

My sister and I drove twenty four hours between us
to bake her a four layer lemon cake
with buttercream icing

and another day in opposite directions
back to our distant lives—and now

in the middle of it, a message on a machine,
word of another death in the family,
and I think I can hear that song.

NOTES

¶ When I visit a new place (or set out to see an old place with new eyes), I make a point of taking a long walk and getting good and lost. Not hopelessly lost, but good and lost. I don't carry a cellphone and never use GPS. I usually carry a map if one is available, but I don't take it out of my pocket unless I find myself crossing the border between good and hopelessly lost. When I get back to my base camp (or some more modern variation), I take the map out and retrace my steps.

Getting lost often takes me to places I'd like to get back to, and retracing steps often reveals connections I wouldn't have found otherwise. Those connections often point to new places to get lost. The whole process, it seems to me, is a good way to make oneself at home if one has a mind to stay.

Notes, tucked away here with the bibliography at the back of the book, are the equivalent of a map in the reader's pocket. If the book is worth reading, there will likely be times when, reading it, you are good and lost. If the territory is challenging enough to be interesting, there may be times when you find yourself crossing the border between good and hopelessly lost. Either way, the map is here for the sake of connections that may take you back to more familiar territory and/or point to new places to get lost.

Please take it out when you need it. And please make yourself at home.

ONE :
A City Out of Thin Air: Politics, Place, Poetry

a lecture presented at the Chicago Cultural Center in September 2009 as part of the First Friday Lecture Series sponsored by the Basic Program of Liberal Education for Adults at the University of Chicago Graham School

¶This first lecture lays down a theme to which I have often found myself returning. It is important, I think, to touch base; and going home is perhaps the most fundamental way to do that. Establishing the rhythm between going home and going away creates a pattern—the rhyme if not the reason—for the dispersed city on which all these lectures dwell.

When I speak in this lecture of "the phenomenologists," I have in mind especially Yi-Fu Tuan but also Maurice Merleau-Ponty, whose meditation on Cézanne has been almost as formative for me as Cézanne's own work.

I've used the original published version of Emily Dickinson's poem (from *Emily Dickinson Edited by two of her friends*, T.W. Higginson and Mabel Loomis Todd. Second Series. Boston: Roberts Brothers, 1891), because that's the version my mother taught me. A more recent "standard" edition of her complete poems is included in the bibliography.

"Politics," by Miller Williams, is from *Imperfect Love*, published in 1986 by the Louisiana State University Press, which has granted permission for it to be reprinted here. It also appears in *Some Jazz a While*, which is included in the bibliography.

"for the light" is included in *a dim sum of the day before* (Temple, TX: Ink Brush Press, 2010).

The discussion of Virginia Woolf uses material that appeared in an earlier form in *Virginia Woolf's Subject and the Subject of Ethics: Notes Toward a Poetics of Persons* (Lewiston, NY: Edwin Mellen Press, 1996).

The oldest surviving map referenced here is discussed (and reproduced) in Warhus, *Another America* (1997).

Though I don't say it directly in the lecture, it is worth considering the possibility implied there that the members of the Long expedition—like Columbus—were *hopelessly* lost.

TWO:
What's Love Got to Do With It?
An Ordinary Song in Ordinary Time

a lecture presented in April 2011 at a Spring Weekend Study Retreat on The Bible: Song of Songs sponsored by the Basic Program of Liberal Education for Adults at the University of Chicago Graham School [translations of Song of Songs are mine unless otherwise indicated]

¶There are many fine English translations of *Shir ha shirim* (in particular those by Chana and Ariel Bloch, Marcia Falk, and Marvin Pope included in the bibliography). But I built this lecture around my own translation because I believe every close reading is a translation of sorts and a careful translation is the closest of close readings (not only as finished product but also as act).

It goes without saying, but since you've pulled out the map you probably expect to see it in writing: this close reading is a meditation on the theme of love introduced near the end of the first lecture. Specifically, it takes up Aristotle's understanding of *philia* as the glue that holds the city together.

My reading of Aristotle's *Nicomachean Ethics*, critical to this lecture as to the others in this series, is shaped by having first read it with Richard Luecke when I was an undergraduate at Valparaiso University. Reading it with Luecke means also reading it with Richard McKeon and John Dewey. That is important for the way I think about *city* in all of these lectures. If built structures are (as Stone suggests) responses to perceived problems, properly posing problems is a key factor in determining the shape of the city—particularly the city (as Luecke would have put it) that *works*.

The reference to Ainsworth and Bowlby points to the *rhyme* of going home/going away with attachment/loss. It might be extended (with Eriksonian undertones) to holding on/letting go and to Piaget's assimilation/accommodation (particularly as Hans Furth read it—with an eye on *desire*—in relation to object formation, formal operations, and the construction of knowledge). The way all these pairs rhyme might shed a little light on the impact of violence on both social and individual identity formation. And the point, it seems to me, is to get a sense of the city as a city of peace, one that abides in spite of forces that threaten to tear it apart.

THREE:

The Halo of a Veil of Tears: On Mysticism and Reason

a revised and expanded version of a lecture presented at the Chicago Cultural Center in October 2011 as part of the First Friday Lecture Series sponsored by the Basic Program of Liberal Education for Adults at the University of Chicago Graham School [another variation on the lecture was presented at the national meeting of the American Academy of Religion in November 2011.]

¶ This third (considerably expanded) lecture is an extended conversation with Bergson and Marx (and, to a lesser extent, Coleridge) shaped in part by my reading of Cornel West's genealogy of pragmatism. Printed sources are included in the bibliography. Readers who want to explore contexts of quoted material in more detail may find these searchable online versions of the central texts particularly useful:

Creative Evolution: archive.org/details/creativeevolutio-ooberguoft

The Two Sources of Morality and Religion: archive.org/details/twosourcesofmora033499mbp

Economic and Philosophic Manuscripts of 1844: marxists.org/archive/marx/works/1844/manuscripts/preface.htm

Critique of Hegel's Philosophy of Right: marxists.org/archive/marx/works/1843/critique-hpr/

Aids to Reflection: archive.org/details/aidstoreflectio-o1marsgoog

Biographia Literaria: gutenberg.org/ebooks/6081

When I was working on the first iteration of this lecture, I was teaching a seminar on Pragmatism in the Basic Program. One of the texts was Cornel West's *The American*

Evasion of Philosophy: A Genealogy of Pragmatism (1989). My students found Brother West's prose difficult, and some argued that it was *too* difficult. That gave me an opportunity to repeat an Aristotelian mantra that I think applies to this lecture as well: *as precise as the subject allows, as difficult as the subject demands.* I find that how much precision a subject allows is often dependent on how much difficulty an inquirer is willing to work through in engaging it. West's genealogy is one of the most precise and thorough available, and it was a precipitating factor in writing a version of this lecture for a panel on prophetic pragmatism at the national meeting of the American Academy of Religion in San Francisco in 2011. West is a structuring absence in the version of the lecture included in this volume. His work (along with that of Douglas Anderson; Eddie Glaude, Jr.; and Joan Richardson) has had a profound influence on the way I read pragmatism.

My conversation with Bergson and Marx is constantly under the influence of Piaget (and Terence Turner's reading of Piaget). Approaching the city as a built structure of built structures means attending to structures of the whole that take place in time. In time, they undergo continual transformation but maintain identity. They are not static structures (though they may have static features) so much as they are dynamic—constructive—processes. And, at bottom, the perceived problem to which organisms (including cities) most urgently respond is the explosive tension that exists between being open and being closed. If an organism is not open to the environment, it dies. If it is entirely open, it disappears.

I come to Bergson by way of Piaget, which involves a step back. A step back, though, is sometimes exactly what is needed to move forward. In this case, I believe Bergson's reading of evolution as a creative process (*sans* Creator) is exactly what is needed to rethink reason as a characteristic of human being in the world. Perhaps the book on Piaget as philosopher will be next—but for now (and perhaps for good), my reading of his philosophy is written between the lines of this lecture.

An earlier version of the discussion of Julian of Norwich was presented at the Southwest regional meeting of the American Academy of Religion. The discussion of John Donne's work draws on a presentation at the Midwest regional meeting of the American Academy of Religion (and on a seminar with students in the Basic Program, whose questions, comments, and careful reading of Donne are much appreciated). The discussion of religion and ethics (beginning with section VI) was published in earlier form in *Santalka* (16/3, 2008.). An earlier version of the discussion of Coleridge appears in *The Metaphysics of Cooperation: A Study of F.D. Maurice* (Amsterdam: Editions Rodopi, 1999). An earlier version of the Bergson material was published (in Russian translation) in a book co-authored with V.M. Pivoev (А. Бергсон и проблемы методологии гуманитарного знания. Петрозаводск: Издательство ПетрГУ, 2008).

FOUR:
The Power of the Powerless

a lecture presented at the Chicago Cultural Center in October 2012 as part of the First Friday Lecture Series sponsored by the Basic Program of Liberal Education for Adults at the University of Chicago Graham School

¶The poem at the beginning of this lecture is the title poem from *Turn* (Virtual Artists Collective, 2012). And it marks a return to the theme with which we began—the dispersed city formed in our going home and going away.

It is also a turn to the ordinary song in ordinary time of the second lecture. The city is a conversation, and conversation is necessarily improvisational. In that sense, it is a sort of song that is subject to interruption; and, at its best, it turns to what is given—what is *there*—and turns it (the way one might turn wood to make something of it). I am reminded of the first of Luther's 95 theses, which asserts that when we are called to turn we are called to make our whole life a life of turning. *To turn and to turn will be our delight...*

In this lecture, thinking about turning turns my attention to the turning of windmills on the plains, built structures that respond to perceived problems of power. And that means another variation on coming and going, recast now as center and periphery. The way wind is turned to power reproduces the centralization of power essential to Capitalism. And that turns us, haunted by Camus, to the power of the powerless.

Two poems lead into the discussion of Havel's essay. The first (haunted by Dylan) turns from a wind farm (the Panther Creek Wind Farm near Big Spring, Texas, for those who want specifics) to a question about the church the world will make of the way the wind is harnessed and a hint of the death of god. The second wonders about the epic opposite, hinting at the two epic traditions—one centered on war, the other on farming—that shape the West.

The poem at the end of section II is the title poem from *we're open, come in* (2014).

The e.e. cummings poem mentioned near the end of the lecture is "why must itself up every of a park..." (available on the Academy of American Poets site: poets.org/poetsorg/poem/why-must-itself-every-park).

The poem with which the lecture ends is "strolling in a time of occupation," from *still* (2015).

FIVE:
A Song of Freedom:
Reinventing the Franciscan Revolution

a lecture presented at the Chicago Cultural Center in October 2013 as part of the First Friday Lecture Series sponsored by the Basic Program of Liberal Education for Adults at the University of Chicago Graham School

¶ Some of the material on Boff and Bonhoeffer in this lecture was presented in an earlier form at the Southwest regional meeting of the American Academy of Religion. This discussion, too, draws on a seminar with students in the Basic Program. My thanks to participants in that lively discussion.

The discussion of Luther's treatise on the freedom of the Christian returns to the theme of conversation as improvisation in the fourth lecture. It is, I think, a reminder of just how closely related Augustinians, Benedictines, and Franciscans are if *hospitality* is taken as the basis of monastic practice. Take the argument seriously (and I think taking it seriously is what made Francis such a threat) and this practice becomes a model of a dispersed city with porous boundaries always open to the stranger. And that is an indication of how closely related monastic practice is to an argument in Judaism that has also been seen as a threat when taken seriously: "be kind to strangers because *you* were once strangers and guests."

The German text of Luther's "Von der Freiheit eines Christenmenschen" is available online: gutenberg.spiegel.de/buch/martin-luther-sonstige-texte-270/6.

An English translation by R. S. Grignon is available on-line at: iclnet.org/pub/resources/text/wittenberg/luther/web/cclib-2.html.

The hermit with whom I turn to Zhuangzi is Thomas Merton, whose *Way of Chuang Tzu* is a wonderful introduction to both Merton and Zhuangzi. (Chuang Tzu and Zhuangzi are alternative transliterations of 莊子.)

SIX:
Everything Out of Its Place: The Work of Poetry

a lecture presented in April 2014 at a Spring Weekend Study Retreat on The Poetry of Robert Frost sponsored by the Basic Program of Liberal Education for Adults at the University of Chicago Graham School

¶Disinterest in making the world "better" coupled with a keen interest in the act is characteristic of American pragmatism. The way it plays out in Frost, I think, has interesting similarities with the way it plays out in John Cage [*Diary: How to Improve the World (You Will Only Make Matters Worse)*]. Neither discourages engagement. Both turn attention from goal to act. *Trying* to change the world (for better or worse) makes about as much sense as *trying* to hit the ground after falling off a cliff. The world will change, and one will hit the ground. Best to focus one's efforts on the (admittedly limited) possibilities of being on the way.

That the possibilities are limited plays a role in the experimental turn suggested in the lecture. Probing limits is one way to identify possibilities and answer the "what is it up to?" question.

During the retreat at which this lecture was delivered, there was an intense discussion of whether Frost was a con artist. It began when, in response to the assertion in another lecture that he wasn't, I suggested that—in a way—he was. Many participants jumped to Frost's defense, though I hadn't meant to attack him and didn't really think he needed defending. At the time, I had in mind the role fools (by which I mean those adept at fooling) play in the shape of history. And I was thinking not only of Shakespeare's characters but also of the con artists and tent preachers I was familiar with from my Texas childhood.

It seems to me that those characters had a remarkable ability to discern what the world was up to at a given time in a particular place (a moment)—and in the best of them that inspired confidence (the con artist's confidence in himself/herself and the mark's confidence in the con artist—but also the mark's confidence in himself/herself). For better or worse, that led a lot of folks to the altar. Playing the fool is one way to inspire playing the fool. And while that may be playing with fire, it may also be the closest thing we have, standing in a place where *wir können nicht anders*, to a gate (whether ivory or horn) by which dreams enter into the world.

My thinking on sonnets, as articulated in this lecture, has been greatly influenced by Paul Friedrich's discussion in *The Language Parallax* (1986).

There is a recording of Cage's *Diary* (five and a half hours in eight parts) online at ubuweb: ubu.com/sound/cage_diary.html. [The text dates from 1967-1972, but the musical performance is from 1991.]

SEVEN:
Unacknowledged Legislators

a lecture presented at the Chicago Cultural Center in October 2014 as part of the First Friday Lecture Series sponsored by the Basic Program of Liberal Education for Adults at the University of Chicago Graham School

¶Reading the exchange between Peacock and Shelley as an instance of fools fooling is the best way, I think, to take it seriously—particularly since Peacock's contribution is routinely ignored and Shelley's is almost always read in isolation as though it were complete and self-contained. Without Peacock's setup, Shelley's essay appears pompous, and the "conclusion" appears delusional. But if Peacock is baiting Shelley (as I think he clearly is)—and if Shelley's response stops in the middle (as it clearly does), that is a different story.

It seems to me that Shelley takes advantage of the setup to begin articulating a theory of cognition that is consistent with the body of his work. And the idea of an *unacknowledged* legislator looks like a serious contribution to psychological theory (anticipating Freud in interesting ways) with promising political implications.

As I suggested in the second lecture, I think the ensemble of human cognition we call "mind" is more nearly analogous to a collection of lyric poems than to a narrative. And Shelley's work is important in making that case. I am willing to make a leap with Plato's Socrates to a close analogy between the structure/construction of the mind and the structure/construction of the city. (One may be a rhyme for the other even if it is not the reason.) In both cases, what turns us plays a major role in determining what we perceive as a problem and how we perceive it. That in turn determines the shape of the cities we build in response.

Some of the material in this lecture was presented in an earlier form at Shenzhen University in 2013. In retrospect, it is interesting to me that the idea of fooling (delivered in English, without translation) didn't fly with an audience that consisted almost entirely of Chinese graduate students and advanced undergraduates. That failure to fly and the questions that it prompted from students and colleagues were most helpful in reshaping the lecture for a Chicago audience.

EIGHT:
What Light Does On Edge

*a lecture presented at the Chicago Cultural Center in October
2015 as part of the First Friday Lecture Series sponsored by the
Basic Program of Liberal Education for Adults at the University
of Chicago Graham School*

¶The "philosopher dog" video is online: youtu.be/s6lE-
otpqaXo.

A good introduction to Land's work can be found in
F.W. Campbell's biography on the Rowland Institute at
Harvard University's website: www2.rowland.harvard.
edu/book/edwin-h-land.

Wendy Carlos has assembled an excellent collection
of material on Land's theory: wendycarlos.com/colorvis/
color.html. I was delighted to stumble upon this resource
because I fell in love with Bach and discovered the Moog
Synthesizer via her *Switched On Bach* not long before I
wandered into Land's theory in high school.

When I speak of looking with O'Keeffe at light edging
onto the plains, I have in mind the series of three watercolors titled "Light Coming on the Plains" in the collection of the Amon Carter Museum of American Art in Fort
Worth, Texas. The collection is searchable online: carter-
museum.org/imu/acm/#imu[browse=enarratives.4433].

The lecture ends with my translation of the first verse
of Laozi's *daodejing*. The translation is part of a collaboration with David Breeden, Mary Ann O'Donnell, Regina
Schroeder, Wally Swist, and Yang Qian that helped me
a great deal in thinking through the ideas addressed in
this lecture—particularly the betwixt and between of the
three parallel translations but also years of conversation

with each of the participants, the play of images in Mary Ann's photos and my paintings, and the chance to work with Regina to bring it all together at the same time that we were putting together the catalog for *dispersed cities*, an exhibit of my paintings (some included in this volume) in Canyon, Texas in March and April of 2015. The collaboration was published by Lamar University Press as *The Daodejing: A New Interpretation* (and I am deeply grateful to Jerry Craven for his support and encouragement).

BIBLIOGRAPHY

Adorno, Theodor W. *Essays on Music*. Translated by Susan H. Gillespie. Commentary and Notes by Richard Leppert. Berkeley: University of California Press, 2002.

Ainsworth, Mary D. Salter, and Bowlby, John, "An ethological approach to personality development." *American Psychologist*, 46, 1991, 331-341.

Anderson, Douglas. *Philosophy Americana: Making Philosophy at Home in American Culture*. Fordham University Press, 2006.

Aristotle. *Nicomachean Ethics*. Aristotle Volume XIX. Loeb Classical Library 73. Trans. H. Rackham. Cambridge, MA: Harvard University Press, 1926.

Aristotle. *Politics*. Aristotle Volume XXI. Loeb Classical Library 264. Trans. H. Rackham. Cambridge, MA: Harvard University Press, 1932.

Augustine. *Confessions*, Translated by F.J. Sheed. Introduction by Peter Brown. Hackett Publishing, 2007.

Bergson, Henri. *Creative Evolution*. Translated by Arthur Mitchell, New York: Dover, 1998 [1911]. [Originally published in French in 1907.]

Bergson, Henri. *Key Writings*. Edited by Keith Ansell Pearson and John Mullarkey. New York: Continuum, 2002.

Bergson, Henri. *The Two Sources of Morality and Religion*. Translated by R. Ashley Audra and Cloudesley Brereton

With the assistance of W. Horsfall Carter. University of Notre Dame Press, 1977 [1935].

Berkeley, George. "Essay towards a new theory of vision" (1709). Etext on Project Gutenberg http://www.gutenberg.org/ebooks/4722. Accessed 7 October 2015.

Berry, Wendell. *The Work of Local Culture*. Iowa City, IA: Iowa Humanities Board, 1988.

Berry, Wendell. *The Unsettling of America: Culture and Agriculture*. Sierra Club Books, 1977.

Blake, William. *Songs of Innocence and of Experience*. Digitized facsimile of the London editions of 1794 and 1826 from copies in the Lessing J. Rosenwald Collection at the Library of Congress. Oakland, CA: Octavo Editions, 2003. Bloch, Chana and Ariel. *The Song of Songs: A New Translation, Introduction, and Commentary*. New York: Random House, 1995.

Boff, Leonardo. *Church: Charism and Power: Liberation Theology and the Institutional Church*. New York: Crossroad, 1986. [Originally published in Portuguese in 1981.]

Boff, Leonardo and Clodovis. *Introducing Liberation Theology*. Orbis, 1988. [Originally published in Portuguese in 1986.]

Bonhoeffer, Dietrich. *Letters and Papers from Prison*. Volume 8 of *Dietrich Bonhoeffer Works*. Edited by Christian Gremmels and John W. De Gruchy. Fortress Press, 2010.

Cage, John, "Lecture On Nothing," in *Silence*. Wesleyan

University Press, 1973.

Cage, John, et al. *Biology and the History of the Future*. Edinburgh University Press, 1972. (An IUBS/UNESCO symposium with John Cage, Carl-Goeran Heden, Margaret Mead, John Papaioannou, John Platt, Ruth Sager, Gunther Stent and C.H. Waddington.)

Cambridge Platonist Spirituality. Edited and Introduced by Charles Taliaferro and Alison J. Teply. Paulist Press, 2004.

Camus, Albert. *The Rebel: An Essay on Man in Revolt*. Translated by Anthony Bower. New York: Alfred A. Knopf, 1954. [Originally published in French in 1951.]

Coleridge, Samuel Taylor. *Aids to Reflection*. The Collected Works of Samuel Taylor Coleridge, Volume Nine. Edited by John Beer. Princeton: Princeton University Press, 1993 [1825].

Coleridge, Samuel Taylor. *Biographia Literaria, or, biographical sketches of my literary life and opinions. The Collected Works of Samuel Taylor Coleridge*, Volume Seven. Edited by James Engell and W. Jackson Bate. Princeton: Princeton University Press, 1983 [1817].

Cummings, E.E. *Complete Poems, 1904-1962*. Edited by George J. Firmage. Liveright, 1991.

Deleuze, Gilles. *Bergsonism*. Translated by Hugh Tomlinson and Barbara Habberjam. Zone Books, 1988. [Originally published in French in 1966].

Deleuze, Gilles. *The Fold: Leibniz and the Baroque*. Translated by Tom Conley. University of Minnesota Press, 1993. [Originally published in French in 1988.]

Derrida, Jacques. *The Gift of Death*. Translated by David Wills. Chicago: University of Chicago Press, 1995. [Originally published in French in 1992.]

Dickinson, Emily. *The Poems of Emily Dickinson*. Edited by Thomas H. Johnson. Boston: Little, Brown and Company, 1961.

Donne, John *The Major Works*. Oxford University Press, 2000.

Falk, Marcia. *The Song of Songs: Love Lyrics from the Bible*. Harcourt Brace Jovanovich, 1977.
[Reissued by Brandeis University Press/University Press of New England, September 2004.]

Foucault, Michel, "The Eye of Power," in *Power/Knowledge: Selected Interviews & Other Writings, 1972-1977*. Edited by Colin Gordon. NY: Pantheon, 1980, pp.146-165.

Freire, Paulo. *Pedagogy of the Oppressed*. NY: Herder and Herder, 1972. [Originally published in Portuguese in 1968.]
Friedrich, Paul. *The Gita within Walden*. Albany, New York: SUNY Press, 2008.

Friedrich, Paul. *The Language Parallax*. University of Texas Press, 1986.

Frost, Robert. *Early Frost: A Boy's Will, North of Boston, and Mountain Interval*. Introduced and Edited by Steven Schroeder. Barnes & Noble, 2009.

Frost, Robert. *The Notebooks of Robert Frost*. Edited by Robert Faggen. Harvard University Press, 2007.

Frost, Robert. *Robert Frost: Collected Poems, Prose, and Plays*. Edited by Richard Poirier and Mark Richardson. New York: Library of America, 1995.

Furth, Hans G. *Knowledge as Desire: An Essay on Freud and Piaget*. Columbia University Press, 1990.

Galileo Galilei. *Sidereus Nuncius, Or the Sidereal Messenger*. Translated by Albert Van Helden. University of Chicago Press, 1989.

Glaude, Eddie S., Jr. *In a Shade of Blue: Pragmatism and the Politics of Black America*. University of Chicago Press, 2007.

Goethe, Johann Wolfgang von. *Theory of Colours*. Translated by Charles Lock Eastlake. Cambridge, Massachusetts: MIT Press, 1970. [Originally published in German in 1819.]

Goldman, Emma. *Living My Life*. 2 vols. New York: Alfred A. Knopf, 1931.

Goyen, William. *Come, the Restorer*. Evanston: TriQuarterly Books/Northwestern University Press, 1996. [Originally published by Doubleday in 1974.]

Gutiérrez, Gustavo. *A Theology of Liberation*. Orbis, 1973. [Originally published in Spanish in 1971.]

Hanson, Norwood Russell. *Patterns of Discovery: An In-*

quiry into the Conceptual Foundations of Science. Cambridge University Press, 1958.

Hartshorne, Charles. *Born to Sing: An Interpretation and World Survey of Bird Song*. Bloomington, IN: Indiana University Press, 1973.

Havel, Václav, et al. *The Power of the Powerless: Citizens Against the State in Central-eastern Europe*. M.E. Sharpe, 1990. [Havel's essay was originally published in Czech in 1978.]

Havel, Václav. *Temptation: A Play in Ten Scenes*. Translated by Marie Winn. New York: Grove Press, 1989 [1985].

Heller, Agnes. *Everyday Life*. Translated by G.L. Campbell. London: Routledge & Kegan Paul, 1984. [Originally appeared in Hungarian in 1970 under the title *A mindennapi elet*.]

Heller, Joseph. *Catch-22*. New York: Simon & Schuster, 1955.

Hoban, Russell. *A Bargain for Frances*. Illustrated by Lillian Hoban. HarperCollins, 1992.

Hoban, Russell. *Riddley Walker*. Washington Square Press, 1980.

Holmes, Urban T. *A History of Christian Spirituality*. Seabury, 1980.

hooks, bell. Yearning: *race, gender, and cultural politics*. Boston: South End Press, 1990.

Ihde, Don. *Listening and Voice: A Phenomenology of Sound.* Athens, OH: Ohio University Press, 1976.

Jakobson, Roman. "Concluding Stattement: Linguistics and Poetics," in *Style in Language.* Edited by Thomas A. Sebeok. MIT Press, 1975.

James, Edwin. *Account of an Expedition from Pittsburgh to the Rocky Mountains, Performed in the Years 1819 and '20, by order of the Hon. J.C. Calhoun, Sec'y of War, Under the Command of Major Stephen H. Long. From the Notes of Major Long, Mr. T. Say, and other gentlemen of the exploring party. Compiled by Edwin James, Botanist and Geologist for the Expedition.* Volume II. Philadelphia: H.C. Carey and I. Lea, 1823.

James, William. *The Principles of Psychology.* Cambridge, MA: Harvard University Press, 1981 [1890].

James, William. *The Varieties of Religious Experience: A Study in Human Nature.* The Modern Library, 1902.

Jelinek, Elfriede. Nobel Lecture 2004, "Im Abseits." Translated as "Sidelined" by Martin Chalmers. *Proceedings of the Modern Language Association* 120/3 (2005): 858–873. http://www.nobelprize.org/nobel_prizes/literature/laureates/2004/jelinek-lecture.html.

Julian of Norwich. *Showings.* Translated by Edmund Colledge, O.S.A and James Walsh, S.J. Preface by Jean Leclerq, O.S.B. Paulist Press, 1978 [c. 1385].

Kandinsky, Wassily. *Concerning the Spiritual in Art.* New York: Dover, 1977. [A republication of the 1914 English translation that appeared under the title *The Art of Spiritual Harmony*. The original German edition, *Über das Geistige in der Kunst*, was published in 1911.]

Kempe, Margery. *The Book of Margery Kempe*. Oxford University Press, 2015.

Kierkegaard, Søren. *Fear and Trembling/Repetition*. Kierkegaard's Writings, VI. Edited and translated, with introduction and notes, by Howard V. Hong and Edna H. Hong. Princeton University Press, 1983. [Originally published in Danish in 1843.]

King, Martin Luther, Jr. *A Testament of Hope: The Essential Writings and Speeches of Martin Luther King, Jr.* Harper Collins, 1990.

Klee, Paul. *Pedagogical Sketchbook*. Translated by Sibyl Moholy-Nagy. Faber & Faber, 1968 [1925].

Land, Edwin H. "Experiments in Color Vision," *Scientific American*, May 1959.

Laozi. *The Daodejing: A New Interpretation*. David Breeden, Steven Schroeder, and Wally Swist. Introduction by Mary Ann O'Donnell and Yang Qian. With photographs by Mary Ann O'Donnell and paintings by Steven Schroeder. Book design by forgetgutenberg.com. Lamar University Press, 2015.

Levitin, Daniel J. *This Is Your Brain on Music: The Science of a Human Obsession*. New York: Dutton, 2006.

Luther, Martin. "The Freedom of a Christian." Translated

by W.A. Lambert. Revised by Harold J. Grimm. In *Three Treatises*. Fortress Press, 1970. [Published in German in 1520.]

Luecke, Richard. "How Cities Talk," in *Liberation and ethics : essays in religious social ethics in honor of Gibson Winter*. Edited by Charles Amjad-Ali and W. Alvin Pitcher. Center for the Scientific Study of Religion, 1985.

Marcuse, Herbert. *One Dimensional Man*. Boston: Beacon Press, 1991 [1964].

Marx, Karl. *The Economic and Philosophic Manuscripts of 1844*. Translated by Martin Mulligan. Progress Publishers, Moscow, 1959. [www.marxists.org/archive/marx/ works/1844/manuscripts/preface.htm]

Marx, K. 2007. Zur Kritik der Hegelschen Rechtsphilosophie. Einleitung (1844), in *Der junge Marx: philosophische Schriften*. Edition linke Klassiker. Ed. by Kraft, S. and Reitter, S. K. K. Promedia Verlag, 109–120. [Karl Marx. *A Contribution to the Critique of Hegel's Philosophy of Right*. http:// www.marxists.org/archive/marx/works/1843/critique-hpr/ [accessed 12 April 2012].

Merleau-Ponty, Maurice. *Sense and Non-Sense*. Translated by Hubert L. Dreyfus and Patricia Allen Dreyfus. Evanston: Northwestern University Press, 1964. [Translation of *Sens et non-sens*, 3rd Edition. Paris: Les Éditions Nagel, 1961. First edition, 1948.]

Merton, Thomas. *The Way of Chuang Tzu*. Second Edition. New Directions, 2010. [The first edition was published in 1965.]

Noë, Alva. *Action in Perception*. MIT Press, 2004.

O'Connor, Flannery. *Three*. New York: New American Library, 1962.

O'Keeffe, Georgia. *Lovingly, Georgia: The Complete Correspondence of Georgia O'Keeffe & Anita Pollitzer*. Edited by Clive Giboire. New York: Simon & Schuster, 1990.

O'Keeffe, Georgia. *Some Memories of Drawings*. Albuquerque: University of New Mexico Press, 1974.

Peacock, Thomas Love. "The Four Ages of Poetry," etext available online at http://www.thomaslovepeacock.net/FourAges.html.

Percy, Walker. "Metaphor as Mistake." *Sewanee Review* 66, 1958, pp.79-99.

Piaget, Jean. *Adaptation and Intelligence: Organic Selection and Phenocopy*. Translated by Stewart Eames. Chicago: University of Chicago Press, 1980. [Originally published in France as *Adaptation vitale et psychologie de l'intelligence: Selection organique et phenocopie* in 1974.]

Piaget, Jean. *Biology and Knowledge: An Essay on the Relations Between Organic Regulations and Cognitive Processes*. Translated by Beatrix Walsh. Chicago: University of Chicago Press, 1971. [Originally published in France as *Biologie et connaissance: Essai sur les relations entre les regulations organiques et les processus cognitifs* in 1967].

Piaget, Jean. *Play, Dreams, and Imitation in Childhood*. New

York: Norton, 1962. [Originally published in France as *La Formation du Symbole* in 1946.]

Piaget, Jean. *The Equilibration of Cognitive Structures.* Chicago: University of Chicago Press, 1985. [Originally published in France as *L'equilibration des structures cognitives: Probleme central du developpement* in 1975.]

Plato. *The Collected Dialogues of Plato, Including the Letters.* Princeton University Press, 1961.

Pope, Marvin H. *Song of Songs: A New Translation with Introduction and Commentary.* The Anchor Bible, Volume 7C. Yale University Press, 1995.

Reed, Edward S. *From Soul to Mind: The Emergence of Psychology, from Erasmus Darwin to William James.* Yale University Press, 1997.

Rich, Adrienne. *What Is Found There: Notebooks on Poetry and Politics.* W.W. Norton, 1994.

Richardson, Joan. *A Natural History of Pragmatism: The Fact of Feeling from Jonathan Edwards to Gertrude Stein.* Cambridge University Press, 2007.

Sartre, Jean-Paul. *Nausea.* Translated by Lloyd Alexander. New Directions, 2007. [*La Nausée* was first published in 1938 by Librairie Gallimard.]

Segundo, Juan Luis, S.J. *The Liberation of Theology.* Orbis, 1976. [Originally published in Spanish in 1975.]

Sheehan, Thomas. *The First Coming.* Dorset Press, 1990.

Shelley, Mary Wollstonecraft. *The Essential Frankenstein.* Wolf, Leonard (Ed.). New York: Plume, 1993. [Originally published in 1818.]

Shelley, Percy. *A Defense of Poetry and Other Essays.* Etext on Project Gutenberg. http://www.gutenberg.org/ebooks/5428. [Written in 1821 and first published in 1840.]

Stallings, A.E. "Triolet on a Line Apocryphally Attributed to Martin Luther," *Poetry Magazine*, April 2005.

Stone, Harris. *Dispersed City of the Plains.* Monthly Review Press, 1998.

Thomas, Larry D. *As If Light Actually Matters: New and Selected Poems.* Texas Review Press, 2015.

Thoreau, Henry David. *Walden.* A digitized version of the first edition (1854) is available at the Internet Archive [archive.org/details/waldenorlifeinwo1854thor].

Tuan, Yi-Fu. *Space and Place: The Perspective of Experience.* University of Minnesota Press, 1977.

Turner, Terence, "Piaget's Structuralism," *American Anthropologist* 75/2 (1973), 351-373.

Udall, Sharyn R. *O'Keeffe and Texas.* San Antonio, Texas: The Marion Koogler McNay Art Museum, 1998.

Unamuno, Miguel de. *Tragic Sense of Life.* Introduction by Steven Schroeder. Translation by J.E. Crawford Fitch. Barnes & Noble, 2006. [Originally published in 1912.]

Warhus, Mark. *Another America: Native American Maps and the History of Our Land.* New York: St. Martin's, 1997.

West, Cornel. *The American Evasion of Philosophy: A Genealogy of Pragmatism.* University of Wisconsin Press, 1989.

Williams, Miller. *Some Jazz Awhile: Collected Poems.* University of Illinois Press, 1999.

Wittgenstein, Ludwig. *Remarks on Colour.* Edited by G.E.M. Anscombe. Translated by Linda L. McAlister and Margarete Schättle. University of California Press, 1978. [Written in 1950.]

Wittgenstein, Ludwig. *Tractatus Logico-Philosophicus.* German text with English translation by C.K. Ogden. Introduction by Bertrand Russell, Routledge, 1922. [First appeared in German in 1921.]

Woolf, Virginia. *Jacob's Room.* New York: Harcourt Brace Jovanovich, 1960 [1922].

Woolf, Virginia. *Mrs. Dalloway.* New York: Harcourt, Brace & World, 1925.

Woolf, Virginia. *To the Lighthouse.* New York: Harcourt, Brace & World, 1927.

Woolf, Virginia. *Orlando.* New York: Harcourt Brace Jovanovich, 1928.

Woolf, Virginia. *A Room of One's Own.* New York: Harcourt, Brace & World, 1929.

Woolf, Virginia. *The Waves*. New York: Harcourt Brace Jovanovich, 1931.

Woolf, Virginia. *Flush*. New York: Harcourt Brace Jovanovich, 1933.

Woolf, Virginia. *Three Guineas*. New York: Harcourt, Brace, Jovanovich, 1938.

Woolf, Virginia. *Between the Acts*. New York: Penguin, 1974 [1941].

Woolf, Virginia. *Moments of Being*. Second Edition. Edited by Jeanne Schulkind. New York: Harcourt Brace Jovanovich, 1985. [Reminiscences (1907), A Sketch of the Past" (1938), 22 Hyde Park Gate" (1920–1921), Old Bloomsbury" (1921–1922), and Am I a Snob?" (1936)]

Wordsworth, William. "Preface," *Lyrical Ballads: Wordsworth and Coleridge*. ed. R. L. Brett and A.R. Jones. London: Routledge, 1991 [1798].

STEVEN SCHROEDER is a poet and visual artist who was born in Wichita Falls, grew up in the Texas Panhandle, studied at Valparaiso University and the University of Chicago (where he earned his Ph.D. in 1982), and spent many years moonlighting as a professor of philosophy and religious studies in Indiana, Iowa, Ohio, Wisconsin, Shenzhen, and Chicago (after a stint in community organizing and social work in Amarillo and Pampa). He has written, co-written, or edited thirty books (though some readers have concluded that it's really thirty variations on a single book). Still fine tuning, he has a new collection of poems (*the moon, not the finger, pointing*), published by Lamar University Literary Press in 2016. More at stevenschroeder.org

www.ingramcontent.com/pod-product-compliance
Lightning Source LLC
Chambersburg PA
CBHW030642020726
47493CB00006B/1825